Presented on April 4, 2016, at the
American Express Leadership
Academy Global Alumni Summit.
New York City, New York

Cultural Intelligence

Cultural Intelligence

CQ: The Competitive Edge
for Leaders Crossing Borders

Julia Middleton

B L O O M S B U R Y

LONDON · NEW DELHI · NEW YORK · SYDNEY

Bloomsbury Publishing Plc
50 Bedford Square
London
WC1B 3DP

www.bloomsbury.com

Bloomsbury is a trademark of Bloomsbury Publishing Plc

Bloomsbury Publishing
London, New Delhi, New York and Sydney

A CIP record for this book is available from the British Library.

ISBN: 9-781-4729-04812

10 9 8 7 6 5 4 3 2 1

Design by Fiona Pike, Pike Design, Winchester
Typeset by Hewer Text UK Ltd, Edinburgh
Printed and bound in Great Britain by CPI Group (UK) Ltd, Croydon CR0 4YY

Contents

Foreword

On my first day at law school, our tutor told us that he could teach us many things about the law, but he couldn't teach us about life. For that, he said, we had to go out into the world and talk to people; to exchange experiences, not just have them.

Now, all these years later, Julia Middleton has written a book about something that she and Common Purpose have been quietly practising everywhere they go: Cultural Intelligence, or CQ.

At its simplest, CQ is a deep and genuine interest in other people, together with the belief that whoever you are and whatever position of influence or leadership you hold, you can learn from them.

As I contemplate this foreword to Julia's book on the subject, the G20 leaders are meeting in St Petersburg. This made me think about whether there is any political leader with any real CQ. These are the people we urgently need to get together and lead the world, but politics is local and domestic, so they struggle to work globally.

Recently, a heavyweight business leader from Australia came to talk to me in Hong Kong. He has huge interests in the region, and he wanted a deeper knowledge of it. No politician ever comes to Hong Kong with that kind of curiosity and willingness to learn about people who are not the ones he serves (with one notable exception, as I will explain).

As the world shrinks and communication accelerates, I believe that CQ is becoming more important, not less. This is because, despite globalisation and the development of new technologies – which makes it much easier to get to know facts and figures, languages and, of course, people – and despite the vast number of diplomats, the increasing number of global institutions and all the opportunities the above have presented to us to make the world a less crazy place, things are, in fact, just as crazy. Leaders will tolerate, and even be diplomatic about, prejudice. They have learned to exercise restraint over the years, but it hasn't got us very far. What we need are leaders who can identify with different situations and be prepared to articulate the issues in a way that brings people together and makes progress.

I am not saying that this is easy: quite the opposite. CQ is human, and it's messy. If you had the most complex Artificial Intelligence computer programme and you fed into it all the economic, political and climatic data the world could assemble, it still could not compute human nature. You can't scan a person's eyeballs to find out what he or she will do or think. In the end, that has to be done at the human level. And human beings are deeply complex. No human being really knows why he or she responds in certain ways, or how we really became what we have become.

So, at a time when information can cross the world electronically in a nanosecond, we are crying out for something as human and imprecise as CQ, which has to be laboriously acquired through human contact. Politics, by its nature, can't deal with this messiness and nor can business. But it is the only way that humanity can make the progress we need.

Whatever CQ that I may have, I learned from my mother. She was Chinese and my father was from the Indian subcontinent. It was, of course, taboo for them to get together, and when I was a toddler, they separated. When I was growing up in Hong Kong, people sometimes asked me, 'What are you?' When I replied 'mixed blood', the response was not generally complimentary. In the end, when I was about six, my mother said to me, 'Ronnie, if you can't accept yourself, no one else will.' It has shaped my basic response to prejudice ever since: 'I am what I am!' Over the years, I have had to learn that IQ was far from the only thing worth having and the only way to get on.

To me, it is entirely fitting that Julia Middleton should take an idea that for the last decade has largely resided in American university research departments and academic papers, and explore it with a whole variety of leaders from all over the world. Because, right from the start, Common Purpose has embodied what CQ stands for.

And we have kept at it: crossing the divides between people in cities and, increasingly, across the world. Persuading different people, from different backgrounds, to believe that they can establish a common purpose and find a way to achieve things that they could not arrive at alone.

Working with Common Purpose in Hong Kong, I have watched career civil servants – bred with the most disciplined traditions of the UK civil service – being thrown among leaders from very different backgrounds who achieve things in different ways. I have watched them go through different experiences and learn to see them through different eyes. And I have seen them genuinely come to believe that there are many ways to make things happen; that theirs is not the only way (or indeed always the best one).

I think that we are all going to look back and wish we had thought about CQ earlier. If we had, we might be in a much better place now. We have left it largely to casual conversations; we haven't worked hard enough at crossing cultures. My generation has been particularly bad in this respect. We have stayed where we were comfortable and have too easily opted out of going where things might be more difficult but deeper, richer progress might be made. Thankfully, younger people are better at it – because we will need them to do much more of it.

Finally, let me give you the notable exception to my earlier assertion that politicians lack CQ. Some years ago, we decided that a good way to recover after Hong Kong was struck by SARS (severe acute respiratory syndrome) was to host a rock concert. Bill Clinton was invited, and he came to a dinner with all the most important people here, including David Tang, the Rolling Stones and Jackie Chan. My son Max was about 10 at the time, and he came, not to meet Clinton, of course, but Jackie Chan. At the dinner, I watched Bill Clinton work the room. He talked to everyone, listened to everyone, asked questions of everyone and everyone knew he was listening to them. He had a deep sense of awareness (I think he must have been born with it) and a gut feeling for the moment, for the act that would draw everyone in the room to him. That night, we all lined up for the obligatory photo of the 'dignitaries'. Suddenly, Bill Clinton shouted, 'Where is Max? He has to be in the picture!' Family and children matter in Hong Kong: it was exactly the right thing to do, for everyone in the room.

As people left that night, they waved across the room to him and shouted, 'See you in DC!' How did he do it and avoid being cheesy?

Perhaps because, for all his power and position, he never got carried away with himself. I can't be sure. I do know that it wasn't put on, and it wasn't prepared. It came naturally, and that's how people responded to it, and to him. He went beyond IQ, and Emotional Intelligence, to CQ.

I hope that this book sheds some much needed light on how to do the same.

Ron Arculli

Senior Partner, King & Wood Mallesons, Hong Kong

Chair of Common Purpose, Hong Kong

Thank you

In writing this book, I have spoken to many people, in many places. How else could a book about Cultural Intelligence be written, when no one person could ever be the authority on it? I have listened as carefully as I could to what they told me about their work, their lives and their experiences, as I tested the ideas I had begun to develop.

I would like to thank them all for their tolerance, their generosity and their willingness to consider a difficult issue. They have allowed me to pick their brains and try out my ideas. Collecting their stories has been wonderful. It has also led to an unconventional structure for the book.

I have quoted a lot of the people I spoke to, at length. Where I had doubts (or changed my mind), I share them. Where people disagreed (with me, or each other), I have kept in all sides of the argument, rather than tidy away things that didn't fit. Where diversion adds richness or depth, I decided to include it.

For reasons that will become clear, this book is a work in progress. It is meant to be the start of a journey, not the last word on it, because that is the nature of the subject. The search for Cultural Intelligence is complicated, messy and without neat resolutions that can be summarised in bullet points.

So, having thanked all the people who helped me, I take full responsibility for the result, for any offence such a book on such an impossible issue may cause, and for the occasionally non-linear nature of the book, which reflects my own messy learning.

I suspect that many of us look around the world and wonder at the mess we see. I believe that this is mostly the result of a failure to communicate, particularly across cultures. I am sure that there are leaders who don't see these problems. I am equally sure that they won't find much in this book to interest them.

I wrote it for leaders who *do* see the problems, even if they despair of finding the answers to them. People who see the sectors – public, private, NGO and everything in between – clashing. People who see all the sub-optimal innovation that results when the same old people get together and come up with the same old answers. People who marvel at the billions spent on developing global brands and organisations, but not in developing the global leaders with the CQ to run them.

This book is for you.

I hope it will help you to cross divides and deliver results. I also hope that the stories and ideas here will weave into your own journey, as they have mine.

Julia Middleton

Introduction

In March 2012, I was in a meeting in Bangalore with a group of leaders from the private, public and community sectors in the city. They told me about a skit they had prepared for leaders who – like them – report to Western bosses.

One person referred to a 'winning' solution for a problem. 'One win?' cried the others. 'Only one? Surely two? A win-win solution it must be. Or, possibly, win-win-win.' The wins accumulated. After all, no Western boss, they declared, could accept a single win. Both must win, all must win (or at least appear to), and all the time. No losing, no giving way, no selling the pass, none of this give-and-take stuff, no muddle-headed-ness. They laughed together as the number of wins mounted up through the skit, with any single win being rapidly corrected to multiple wins.

'It's how to keep Westerners happy,' they told me. Western bosses are wary of wins in single figures and, more importantly, the poor aspiring leaders who might either propose them or settle for them. One of the group then went on to suggest that there were three options for ways forward on an issue. The others howled again: 'Three? How could there possibly be *three*?! You must be mistaken,' they exclaimed. Mistaken, or confused, or disorganised: muddle-headed again. 'There can only be two options: one right, the other wrong. Only two are allowed.' 'Oh yes, of course, forgive me,' said the first speaker. 'Of course, two. This one, and that one. Just two, so sorry.'

Western bosses distrust more than two, they explained to me. They like and trust two crystal-clear alternatives. Good luck to you if there are more. Two options are, apparently, what any clear-minded leader will give you, in all circumstances. Fear for the poor individual who suggests more than two clear ways forward on any issue.

As they spoke, they began to nod and shake their heads incessantly. Not like leaders normally do in India to reinforce a point, but exaggerated shaking: maniacally throwing their heads from side to side and up and down as they caricatured themselves with confidence. They were laughing at how – as they well know – Western bosses find Indian head-nodding so very silly.

I laughed and nodded too, and struggled to understand and to respond. They laughed with such confidence as they gave each other examples – lots of them – of situations when they had met with these responses from their Western bosses. They had no doubt whatsoever that their observations rang true.

Meanwhile, I was trying hard to get my head around how the world had changed. How I belonged to the ridiculed group. How delicious it was to see such confidence. How nervous I would feel if I caricatured leaders from India in this way. So why was it OK for them to ridicule my culture? Is simply turning the tables a good enough reason? Was it a good sign or a bad one that they would share such insights with me? And I wondered if my fellow Westerners realised just what their colleagues in India thought of them.

Then, just a few weeks later, I met with leaders from an Australian company. They identified a problem which needed fixing and said that they would put a 'Black Head' on to it. Curious, I asked what the phrase meant. Someone Asian, they responded, without a moment of hesitation. I stared at them; it takes a moment to take in phrases like that. While I stared, they kept talking. They were clearly not proposing to put someone less effective on to the task. They wanted someone quick, fast, analytical, with a good eye for detail. Someone in the middle ranks, a low-cost person, a process person. Someone among the many (they have lots of 'Black Heads') who clearly eat up work.

When I then questioned the expression, I got a very heavy push-back: 'Let's not get all politically correct here, shall we?', they said. 'Let's not bring your Old World angst in now, Julia. Black Heads are great guys and they don't mind being called Black Heads.'

Wherever you go in the world, stories like these abound. People are being thrown together, and are struggling to adapt and get on. Old and new divides are being crossed, hurling geographies, faiths and beliefs together. It's happening with sectors too; the boundaries are blurring between the public, private and NGO sectors and leaders are struggling to understand one another, however great the rewards may be for doing so.

The balance of cultures is shifting, merging, clashing. I think that in this New World the leaders who will be prized are those who can cross – and connect – cultures. Leaders who understand multiple worlds, who can cope with their own mistakes and even enjoy being teased for them. Leaders who can resonate among people who are very different from themselves. Leaders who are prepared to unpick what they have been doing forever, and, in so doing, bravely and legitimately face head-on the issues that emerge, rather than shying away from hearing or saying difficult things. How sought-after they will become. They will have Cultural Intelligence. It's not an oxymoron: the two words can belong together.

So I thought I would write a book about the Cultural Intelligence I have seen in the small number of leaders I have met who I think have it (or at least have more of it than most of us). It will be a naive book, almost by definition. Firstly, because I am a white, Western, straight woman of Christian origin. I see issues through my own 55-year-old eyes, however open I hope they are. But, then again, perhaps no one can ever really have the proper legitimacy to write about CQ, however important it is to try in today's world. And secondly, because what I write will be based on what I know now. Learning about leadership is a long journey. Writing this book has certainly taught me more about the CQ that I believe leaders need. It has changed how I behave and do things. Six months from now, for sure, I will know even more and change further. And I will wish that I could write this book all over again.

Speaking to so many people has been fascinating. With some of them, however, I did not always enjoy hearing what was said, and I am still finding some things very difficult to digest, rethink and turn into action. I invite you – as you read on – to give me feedback. And on good days, when I can take it, I shall read it, and change some more.

Part One

What is Cultural Intelligence (CQ)?

I believe that Cultural Intelligence (CQ) is the natural evolution from the now well-established notions of Intelligence Quotient (IQ) and Emotional Intelligence (EQ). It is an essential ingredient for leaders who recognise that they can no longer be, to quote John Donne, 'an island, entire of itself'. And it will be crucial to the success of the organisations they lead: companies, communities, cities, countries and continents.

All these leaders will need to acquire CQ if they are to be successful in the world as it is today. And they will need to acquire it through experience: slowly, honestly, carefully and sometimes painfully, because there is no other way to do it. In the future, I suspect that organisations will continue to recruit heavily for IQ (things won't change that fast). And they will still sometimes fire employees for having a lack of EQ, as so many do now. But, increasingly, what they will promote for is CQ.

IQ

IQ testing was developed by French psychologist Alfred Binet in the early 1900s and became very popular in the USA when his work was translated there in 1910. Ever since then, it has dominated our sense of personal worth. IQ is what has allowed us to pass exams, get jobs and then be promoted. It has given us respect, and pride. It proves our ability to master a brief, to sort out complex concepts, to present ourselves as coherent and on top of facts, systems and arguments.

Parents are proud of clever children. I remember, even when my children were tiny babies, I would love to point out something they did that clearly (to me anyway) indicated what a high IQ they would eventually have. They were sure to end up in the top quartile of some sort.

IQ is undoubtedly a crucial ingredient, particularly if you are going to lead thought, research, markets, analytics or consultancy. And if you are going to lead people, IQ matters too. If nothing else, it speeds things up. But it leaves some leaders helpless when they are faced with the increasing number of calls – not decisions, but fine calls – that have to be made with either no data or an overload of data, when they will have to turn to an assessment of people. My children laughed when they heard my response to their question 'Where were you when Dad asked you to marry him?' My answer? 'On my knees trying to get him to make a decision without needing to define love.'

IQ matters. But, for leaders of people, it's only a starting point. Vidya Shah is a successful investment banker in Mumbai who now runs the EdelGive Foundation. She puts it very well: *'Brains: it is what we admire. Analytical brains. We punish people who don't get the point fast enough. We want smart people: smart at numbers and arguments (even if they make everyone around them feel insecure). It slips off the tongue, to ask what grades people got. It's not what we always need: but we still put it up there as the highest priority, and it is at our peril.'* Etienne de Villiers is a very successful South African businessman. He has worked in global media and sports businesses, from the ATP Tour, to Walt Disney International TV, to BBC Worldwide. He makes the warning even starker: *'If you are highly analytical, the thing you have to resist is the need to get your point heard. This gets in the way of listening. People with high IQ think their role is to share their knowledge and analysis. They have to stop doing this and turn the transmitter from 8 to 2 and the receiver from 2 to 8.'*

EQ

Since the 19th century, many other forms of intelligence have been identified. In 1872 Charles Darwin wrote about what we now know as emotional-social intelligence as a strategy for survival in *The Expression of the Emotions in Man and Animals*. And, in 1983, American psychologist Howard Gardner recognised seven distinct types of intelligence in his book *Frames of Mind: The Theory of Multiple Intelligences*.[1] But the form that entered everyone's consciousness is EQ, largely as a result of Daniel Goleman's 1996 international bestseller *Emotional Intelligence*.[2] Chambers Dictionary defines Emotional Intelligence as 'The ability to perceive and assess the emotions of oneself and of others.' I wanted to learn more about the groundbreaking effect of the book on our understanding of leadership. Jonathan Donner, Head of Leadership Development for Unilever, explained it to me like this: '*The book was groundbreaking at the time. It gave legitimacy to the study of people, rather than facts. The "art" of leadership, rather than the "science" of leadership. In the West, it well and truly knocked IQ off the high altar. IQ was suddenly one of the ingredients for a leader – and not the essential one. Look at education policy ever since. Look at leadership programmes ever since. And, even more, look at appraisal systems. The book suggested that very clever people would not automatically be very good leaders. In fact, it even suggested that IQ might sometimes get in the way.*'

At first, I must confess, I found EQ miserable, because it was what women were supposed to have. It rapidly became associated with 'soft (i.e. female) skills'. Emotion was what women were supposed to do better than men. As the only woman on many panels about leadership, I could always feel the questions approaching, working their way towards me. I was almost always the last panel member to be invited to comment on an EQ question. I suppose the chair felt that I was being given the final say. So the questions sort of wound their way to me, as the oracle on the soft skills of EQ, simply because I was the woman in the room. With an encouraging smile, I would be asked for my 'female – more emotional – take on leadership'. I seldom made much sense. This was largely for three reasons. One, because I was so bad-tempered; two, because I wanted my sons to develop EQ and for it not to be perceived as feminine to do so; and three, because it is such a ridiculous idea that understanding people is in some way 'soft' and understanding facts is 'hard'. There is nothing soft about understanding people, it's hard, and when you get it wrong, it is very, very hard indeed.

Even more dispiriting, the word 'emotional' was also sometimes prefixed – especially by people who preferred the certainty and measurability of IQ – with the word 'over'. The unspoken fear was that we would end up with over-emotional leaders, short on IQ, who would produce irrational thinking. Almost as if 'emotional' and 'intelligent' were words that could not sit comfortably beside each other in the same sentence, let alone the same person.

Things have moved on since then. Nowadays, we know that not all women have EQ. And that, fortunately, many men have a lot of it. Though I sometimes wonder if some men still have to hide their EQ a little, for fear of being perceived as feminine, soft, even 'over- emotional'.

Now, almost all leaders know they need some EQ. They certainly know that IQ is not enough to lead effectively. After all, the ability to understand people, and – crucially – to be *interested enough* in people to learn to understand them, seems to me to be a pretty essential prerequisite for leading them. However, people in India often tell me that – even now – they still recruit leaders mainly for IQ and then end up firing them for their lack of EQ. Sadly, in the pursuit of IQ, the broader and more experiential learning that delivers EQ too often gets missed out.

Having been a highly successful banker in London and New York, Peter Kulloi is now a venture philanthropist in his home city of Budapest. He also described to me the effect of reading the EQ book: '*It was very important. It articulated and gave respectability to something that many people had felt for a long time. I knew it from my biology teacher in 1977, when I was 17. She told me that intelligence came in four parts: cleverness, the ability to remember, emotional richness and Alkalmazkodóképesség.*' Which, Peter tells me, literally means 'adaptability' in English. In Hungarian, however, it's a much richer word: '*It conveys warmth and proactiveness. It is not just about adapting, but rather more adopting – and adopting with delight.*' So Peter's biology teacher had anticipated EQ for him, long before Daniel Goleman pinned it.

CQ

But now, as I look at the interconnected world around us, I think we need something more than EQ. I think it is increasingly important to be able to communicate – fully – with people from different cultures. And I don't just mean different countries: I mean cultures. Look up the word 'culture' in the Chambers Dictionary and you get this definition: 'The attitudes and values which inform a society'. I would extend it to include sectors, organisations and generations too. I think that the process of properly understanding another culture requires a great deal more than a map and a phrasebook. It requires Cultural Intelligence.

The concept of CQ emerged in academic research in American universities some time ago. Since then, it has been hailed as a way for corporations to sell in new markets, and for military forces to operate more effectively on foreign soil. People have suggested that you can measure it, like IQ. There are even online self-assessments that aim to 'improve your CQ score'. I believe that the whole subject is bigger and more complicated than this.

I think CQ is needed wherever cultures clash and problems go unsolved, and I think there is really only one way to acquire it and develop it. This is why I decided to write this book. My inspiration, at least in part, is Bill George, Professor of Management Practice at Harvard University. In my view, he has leapfrogged the conventional academic notion of what CQ is and has given it a properly global perspective. He defines the world as Volatile, Uncertain, Chaotic and Ambiguous (VUCA), and he suggests that, in order to be effective in such a world, leaders must develop a VUCA response: Visionary, Understanding, Clarity and Adaptable. His overall description of this is Global Intelligence (which he shortens to GQ).

I find this inspiring. But, as I have said, I believe that Cultural Intelligence is about more than bridging national borders and developing your capability to operate globally. It is about crossing all kinds of cultural borders, learning to operate effectively in unfamiliar surroundings and finding a way to break down barriers that may well not be geographical at all. In my view, the best global leaders will need to be able to do this too.

Similarly, CQ is often confused with 'diversity'. The 'diversity' agenda has come to be dominated by the idea that it is about minorities and majorities and how they interact with each other. For some people, diversity therefore becomes a simple numbers game. Again, for me, this does not go far enough. We are all part of a majority of some kind, and we are all often part of a minority of some kind. As many of the people I spoke to while I was writing this book prove, it is possible to be in a majority and a minority at the same time. And, as you move between cultures and sectors and countries, the balance can be constantly changing.

So, for me, CQ is not about numbers. It is really about individuals. At its simplest, I would define CQ as the ability to connect across cultures. But I believe that it is actually the ability to go across cultural divides – and thrive there. Leaders with CQ don't shy away from difference; they gravitate towards it. They prefer to be in a world that is heterogeneous, rather than homogeneous. They don't see heterogeneity as threatening; they see it as creative, exciting, inspiring and enriching. They don't insist that a team can only be built on everyone agreeing with each other, or looking like each other or thinking like each other. Quite the opposite.

Leaders with CQ can move across all the divides, old and new, and do it with ease. East and west; north and south; developed and developing; able-bodied and disabled; men and women; tall and short; wealthy and struggling; swanky and unswanky; atheist and believer; deep faith and all faiths; government and corporate; left and right; rational and emotional; commerce and community; old and young.

What's more, they don't simply cross the boundaries. They also understand what is going on when they get there. They are streetwise: on both sides of the street, and wherever the street takes them. After a career running Dubai-based Air Cargo Trader, Issa Baluch is now a Senior Fellow at the Advanced Leadership Initiative at Harvard University. He defined it for me in the same way: '*CQ is being street-smart in lots of cultures. I have loved being at Harvard, but this kind of street-smart is what the students need.*'

Sir John Parker, Chairman of Anglo American plc, describes the same ability, but in a different way: '*We have an expression in Northern Ireland: "people who can hear the grass growing". They can sniff the air and feel what's happening. They can navigate through the cabbage patch and have an instinct for how to react.*' Sitting in his London office, looking out over St James's Park, we asked each other: what is the global equivalent?

Bill George at Harvard would probably say GQ. I think the answer is CQ. I also think that John Parker might have been wrong to use the word 'instinct'. It might well feel like instinct to the people who have it, but I think it comes from experience, partly of different places, but mainly of different people. That is why CQ is harder to acquire than IQ: and a step on from EQ.

This book has lots of examples of what I mean by CQ, but here's a story that shows what can happen when someone who really needs it doesn't have it. Recently, I discussed CQ with a friend who is the Chief Executive of a large international company. This is the story he told me to illustrate his take on it: '*Our new Chairman was brought up in the UK. He has chaired many UK companies, but he has no international experience – and it shows. As a board, we went to visit a company in Asia Pacific with which we were in a joint venture. He was truly awful. He spoke in rapid English, to middle managers whose English was not strong, and he talked at them. He used Western management-speak. He picked up nothing from their presentation, and never referred to it in his. Everything he said referred back to the UK. He made people feel different, rather than part of something collaborative, and they all nodded back, because they did not want him to lose face. As a result, he thought they had all got on fine. It was deeply embarrassing that such an experienced operator who was Chairman of such a big company could be so poor at CQ.*'

Leaders who have CQ don't just cross the divides, they also build bridges for others to use. That is how they counterbalance the herding instinct that drags everyone back towards homogeneity: the default human preference for talking and working and sticking with 'people like me'.

I well remember speaking at a conference for a global organisation several years ago. I was addressing the 'two years in' generation of talent on the subject of leadership. They were exciting and fun, but very, very 'samey'. They mostly looked the same, they nodded when one of them asked a question, they laughed together and were quiet together at the same moments and they all seemed excited by the same things. I commented on it at the time: and assumed that this was why they didn't invite me back the following year. Then, some years later, they did. They even referred to my original comment in the invitation, and said that the audience would look very different now, and they did. Men and women, visibly from all over the world: it was very exciting. Then we got to the question session, and it became clear that, while the company had been bold in its recruitment, they had also ironed out all the differences pretty fast. 'Group-think' had set in within two years. They were all 'samey' again. This time round, they just didn't look it.

Leaders with CQ go the other way. They go outwards. They are excited by different cultures, not alarmed by them. They don't just tolerate difference, they actively *enjoy* it. They trust it, make it a strength and thrive on it. In the process, they also share their enthusiasm, so that it becomes infectious, and that's how CQ spreads.

Are they sequential?

So far, we have looked at IQ, EQ and CQ as a logical sequence. This is partly because they represent a historical progression, from Alfred Binet, to Daniel Goleman and Bill George, to now. And there is an argument for keeping the progression in mind as we explore CQ: not least because the roadblocks along the way shed light on why CQ is so valuable.

Leaders with IQ can cope with a vast amount of complicated (and usually competing) information, and they are excellent at putting it – and keeping it – in order. Leaders with high IQ recognise that they cannot take people out of the equation, and they move on to add EQ to their toolkit. Leaders with EQ understand people, but often the people they understand are people who are similar to them. Leaders with high EQ recognise that they have to go beyond understanding people 'like me' to engage with people who aren't like them at all, and that's where CQ comes in.

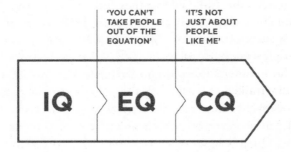

'YOU CAN'T TAKE PEOPLE OUT OF THE EQUATION'   'IT'S NOT JUST ABOUT PEOPLE LIKE ME'

IQ > EQ > CQ

Diversions and dead ends

If we assume that this progression is a straight road (we'll come back to that), there are dead ends all the way along it. And, consciously or unconsciously, many leaders happily go down them, never to return. I discussed this with Di Schneider, who is Head of Strategic Talent and Transformation at Deloitte & Touche in South Africa. She describes leaders with high IQ who have convinced themselves that IQ is all they need, and go around saying, *'If we could just take the people issues out of this problem, it'd be so much easier to solve.'* How many times have we all heard this? With a sinking heart, as you realise that you've reached the deadest of dead ends? Of course these leaders have their place, but it is a smaller place than they might think. Sir Graham Boyce is a former British Ambassador now on the board of several multinational corporations. He is, to me, the epitome of IQ (and, in his case, a great deal more). His view? *'What so many clever people get wrong is to assume that all people are reasonable, like them. But you have to be prepared to understand things that you may well consider unreasonable – and accept them. That's what the really clever leaders do.'*

Then there are leaders with IQ and EQ, who get so convinced that they are good with people that they stop making any effort. Back to Di Schneider: *'Yes, IQ can be a dead end, but so can EQ, especially if it leads people to complacency. They're perfectly happy surrounded by people like them; but they're actually stuck.'* I call this 'cultural stuckness', and I'd argue that people who suffer from it are unlikely to go much further as leaders.

I met the remarkable Mike Brearley a few months ago. I don't know or understand cricket, but I know that, in the 1980s, Mike captained one of the most successful England cricket teams, including two of the best individual players ever to play the game. I also know that his success famously lay in his extraordinary leadership skills. After he retired from cricket, Mike trained as a psychoanalyst, and he is now a Fellow of the Institute of Psychoanalysis. I went to see him to pick his brains on CQ. With that gentle, generous sideways smile, he said that he was fatally flawed on CQ because, by definition, he had only ever led men. But, after a deal of pushing on my part, he did share a definition of leadership that has gone deep with me. He said that the role of a leader is to *'comfort the troubled, and trouble the comfortable'*.

Why do the comfortable need troubling, I asked him? *'Because they get smug, set in their ways, hearing only the voices they choose to hear, not trying anything new, not gathering all the talent, not seeing the enormous world that they don't know. They stop travelling: physically and mentally. They have no need for CQ, because they are comfortable where they are, and they simply stop getting better.'*

There are two further dead ends looming here. Leaders who simply can't imagine that there is anyone who isn't like them, or worse, leaders who are perfectly aware that such people exist – but don't want anything to do with them. The first is cultural ignorance. The second, cultural intolerance. Both lead to blind spots, and both make it impossible for leaders to complete the transition from EQ to CQ. We'll come back to them later.

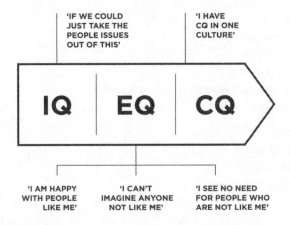

Even when you get into CQ, there is another potential roadblock. I discussed this with Sir Eric Thomas, now Vice-Chancellor of Bristol University, who, early in his career, spent several years working in Japan, learning to operate in a culture very different from his own. The experience can be a way into CQ, but, as he pointed out, it can also be another dead end if you're not careful: *'The question is, how do you take what you learn from experiencing another culture and apply it to all "other" cultures? So that you can pick up what is going on in a room – be sophisticated, alert, aware, sensitive – even if you have not lived in that specific culture? How do you take the*

experience in one country and translate it across many?' That's what this book is about, and I wouldn't stop at countries. CQ is not just about crossing time zones; it's about crossing cultural dividing lines wherever they occur; between generations, between sectors, between tribes of all kinds.

One final twist

So far, so sequential. A straight road from IQ to EQ to CQ, with some diversions to avoid on the way. But, as ever with CQ, nothing is quite that simple. I discussed it with Philip Yang, Procurement Director at GlaxoSmithKline in China, and for him, my neat sequential progression fell at pretty much the first hurdle. In fact he laughed, and told me that I had finally helped him to find a piece of CQ he had been looking for in order to understand some of the Western business people with whom he had been struggling to work: *'I think, in China, EQ and CQ come before IQ. Our society is based on relationships. I find it very difficult being endlessly asked for facts by my Western bosses. They love facts. And, when I negotiate with Western suppliers, I struggle to cope with the numbers they bring me. They go on and on showing me facts and figures; they don't understand that the deal will be done based on the relationship we establish.'*

My conclusion? It isn't always a sequential journey from IQ to EQ to CQ. In fact, in some parts of the world, it's quite the opposite. And Mike Brearley needn't worry: there's little chance here of the comfortable avoiding getting troubled in the search for CQ.

---

1. Gardner, Howard. *Frames of Mind: The Theory of Multiple Intelligences.* New York: Basic Books, 1983.

2. Goleman, Daniel. *Emotional Intelligence.* London: Bloomsbury Publishing, 1996.

Part Two

Why do I need CQ?

I believe that CQ has found its moment. We have never needed it more than we do right now. Shifts are taking place globally that call for – indeed demand – leaders with CQ. These changes are also happening locally, in cities and communities all around the globe. I think there are eight of these changes. There may well be more, but here are my eight that say the time for CQ has come.

The need for collaboration

Big problems can no longer – if they ever could – be solved by one person, one sector, one culture, one community, one country or even one continent, operating alone, so leading across boundaries through collaboration is increasingly crucial. The problems faced by organisations require their separate divisions – production, sales, marketing, finance – and their leaders to collaborate. Cities need the public, private and not-for-profit sectors to find ways to work more effectively together, if they are to use their resources and assets to best effect. Countries and continents face global problems of an order that requires old and new divides to be crossed.

Yet most leaders spend the bulk of their time operating within the boundaries of their division, their sector or their nation. And, for the most part, they learn to lead in such circumstances, with a defined, agreed and established role, and commensurate budget and accountability, where what they say and do comes with some authority. How heavily or lightly they choose to use this authority is up to them, but they still have it, and everyone knows they have it. They have been encouraged to focus on the area they are accountable for, and they know they will be judged on what they achieve within it. They also know that they are likely to be told to stick to their own knitting ('mêle-toi de tes oignons', as I was told in France) if they stray from it. This ill-prepares them to deal with problems that cross boundaries, or to work with people over whom they have no authority, and of whom they have little understanding.

A very senior leader in a global firm recently told me a not untypical story: *'When it was suggested that I work with stakeholders in government, I thought my CEO had gone mad. I told him to send someone from Government Affairs. But, apparently, if the project we were working on was going to happen, I would have to be the person who led it, and in collaboration – that fatal word. My whole career had told me that bureaucrats and collaboration were things to be avoided as time-wasting and tedious. The trouble was that my CEO was right. The project would stall – however clever the plan – without working with the stakeholders, and I don't just mean the government.*

To start with, it was a nightmare. Every time I wanted to make something happen, to drive through a decision, I was told I was being overbearing; I was forever offending someone or other. Their jargon was like another world – and they accused me of using jargon! I ended up doing a lot of table thumping, but to no great effect. After a while, I began to realise that, though my ideas were almost certainly the best way forward, the way I went about things guaranteed that we would never get them into play. I suppose I have had to learn to finesse; to pace, to listen, to have – aaargh – patience. To see that I, too, have my own jargon. To appreciate others' constraints, and find ways around them. To appreciate that some other people have different ways of doing things that are not worse or weaker, just different. And sometimes, maybe, even better. When you are used to things being linear, your first response to complexity can be that it is the product of poor decision-making – untidy thinking and planning. Collaboration has slowed us down, for sure; but I think maybe it has given us a more lasting outcome. I can't say that I have become someone who enjoys this. But I can only thank the rest of the team for having the patience and commitment to see it – and me – through. It's a project that I am now very proud of. But asking me to work in collaboration was like asking a fish – albeit a well-trained and effective fish – to walk. It is very hard. It can be done, but it's very hard. The upside (apart from the successful project) has been that I thump the table less in my main job now too.'

Leaders are having to learn to lead through collaboration and to work with people over whom they have no, or even minus, authority. With this comes the requirement to work with people from different cultures and backgrounds and of different ages. People who leaders don't understand, or know whether to trust. People who are difficult, sensitive, touchy, even hurt. People who can be precious on occasions: rude, offensive or simply confused. In some cases, people who really, really don't want to work with you.

Adam Habib is a professor of political science and Principal of the University of the Witwatersrand in Johannesburg. We invited him to speak about CQ at the Study Conference for Commonwealth Leaders (CSCLeaders) run by Common Purpose in South Africa in June 2013. He highlighted the importance of genuine co-operation, however hard it may be: *'Polarisation doesn't work, so leaders have to start cutting deals. They have to learn to concede, and see issues through other people's lenses. And they sure look different. Take for example the global debate on whether to intervene in conflict countries:*

> *"Let's go in, no-fly zone, close the guy down; he is trying to kill his citizens."*
> *"Don't compromise national sovereignty under any circumstances."*
> *"How can you worry about national sovereignty when people are dying?"*
> *"We survived the colonialists for hundreds of years; don't lecture us about national sovereignty."*

And so a debate about regime change brings back to the surface a debate about colonialism that you didn't see coming. I promise you that if you hear that there is one answer to any problem you shouldn't trust it: you are probably just not seeing the other angles. Almost everything is about understanding the tensions, and managing them. If you can't deal with tensions, then stop trying to lead. It's simple: if you don't see things through multiple lenses in the modern world, you will fail.'

You see the same shifting priorities within organisations, between sectors and across national borders. R Gopalakrishnan is an Executive Director of one of the largest Indian business groups, Tata Sons. I discussed with Gopal the changing nature of the relationships involved in running the company: *'In the old days, some forty years ago, all company leaders had to understand were their own organisation and industry, and, to a considerable extent, the Indian government. Today, in addition to all these, they also have to understand the leaders of civil society, both in India, and from around the world. Civil society was not an expression my generation had to consider seriously during decision-making in business matters. Today, if you get the links with civil society wrong, you simply can't do business. So our leaders today and tomorrow need to be able to adapt to new cultures in ways that they have never had to do before, and in places they have never had to do it before.'*

It is not confined to single organisations. You see it in societies too. Arun Maira, formerly Chairman of Boston Consulting Group in India, is now a member of the Planning Commission of India: *'It is not easy to get the sectors to work together, even when you gather them for a very compelling cause. I was part of an effort to get the public, private and NGO sectors together on the issue of malnutrition in India. Despite our economic success, India has failed to make much progress on this issue. I would describe it almost as an unwillingness to be in the same room. Corporate leaders are focused on pointed professional management: they see the public sector as over-questioning, over-complicating and indecisive, and they see the NGO sector as good news, but delivering unquantifiable results. The behaviour of the corporate sector is then accentuated, because they have been put on a pedestal for some time now across the world. They are almost treated like a superior tribe, and, as a result, they behave like one, which limits their ability to participate. Then there is the government sector. They feel hammered: they are told that they are inefficient and that no one trusts them, and this has led to them feeling inferior. And then the NGO sector is full of passion: to the point of not hearing any other voices. How would I do it differently next time (because there will be a next time, the need to work together is so compelling)? At the opening of the session, I would not welcome them to a tri-sector meeting. I should have said "there are no sectors here today, just people". And I would speak to each of the participants in advance, and ask of them two things:*

1. *To remember that they came to the meeting in the hope of leaving with a new understanding from the one they arrived with. For this to happen, there will need to be new ideas discussed which they don't have already, and these ideas will come from other people, so they must listen from the start.*

2. *To prepare themselves to hear things that they have heard before. And, when they do, not to go – mentally and physically – into "I have heard this all before" mode. Because, if they do, the person speaking will pick up their lack of respect and respond to it accordingly, and, slowly but surely, all will spiral inexorably downwards.'*

Maria Figueroa Kupcu, a partner at communications firm Brunswick in New York, sees the same problem from the other side of the world, and adds: *'The friction between the sectors often emanates from differences in pace and expectations of time horizons. Corporates have laid out a plan. They want to follow that, get through the steps and move on. Communities have been here for hundreds of years, and know nothing will change fast. So one side irritates the other. One cries, "You are slowing us all down" and the other shouts back, "You are rushing us". If either side even so much as acknowledges this issue, it can prompt the other to start building bridges, but it's rare.'*

These are all examples of people operating in parallel universes, or like ships passing in the night, unable to understand each other's points of reference and vocabulary, let alone find common ground to create co-operation. All these situations call for CQ. Without it, leaders will lead underperforming collaborations where two and two struggle to add up to one, or the collaborations will simply never get off the ground, as people go their own way. Silos will go unbusted, sectors will continue to clash, resources will be wasted, divides will deepen and the big problems will simply stay unsolved.

The reality of networks

The world is becoming more connected. At the same time, institutions are being questioned, organisations are becoming flatter and social networks are burgeoning as never before. Leaders know it is happening, and they know they must build networks in order to cope with it all – and capitalise on the opportunities it presents. There will always be a role for networks of people 'like me': to give leaders encouragement, reinforcement and support. But 'like me' networks will always be of limited value for leaders who also want to see what others see and to cross boundaries to work effectively with people who are very different. These leaders need to develop what I call 'turbulent networks' to give them a counterbalancing discomfort, distance and sometimes even dissonance. And, for that, they will need CQ.

I came across the epitome of turbulent networks recently in Turkey. Imagine two women. One a dentist, a posh extraordinarily expensive dentist. The other, the president of an Islamic women's network. One who shows flesh wherever she can. The other covered, but for her face. One with long, shaped, fabricated, painted and polished nails. The other with short, clipped nails. Both hugely elegant: one with Prada and Gucci, the other with deep colours, beautiful leather and rich materials. One who steps up to grab every single opportunity, relishing the limelight. The other who would never put herself forward. Both hugely effective in everything they do. One is a showwoman: it's not just an act, she wants to be popular – and is. The other is quiet and would never do anything extravagant. One trusts first, the other trusts last. When either woman speaks, others listen intently, their voices are at opposite ends of the volume spectrum. One has a driver, the other drives a Jeep. They meet privately because the friends of both would find their friendship deeply incongruous. Neither would make any serious decision without seeking the input of the other. Sometimes they say that they would like to "choke each other"; but they both say that they can "see each other's true heart".

I discussed networks like this with Paula Marra, co-founder and Director of Argentinian agribusiness company Grupo Los Grobo. The idea of turbulent networks is firmly established in their corporate culture, from the top: *'Almost the first lesson we learnt in the Board of Directors of our company was to develop what you call turbulent networks for ourselves and for the whole board. We made an intelligent and conscious effort to build them, and to learn to listen. To understand what emotions and feeling were involved in our judgements, and also what beliefs and cosmovisions. I believe that the more different the thinking you can gather, the better the solutions you come up with, and this is why we survived as a company. We became a network. We adapted to our own environment, like an amoeba. If an idea works, we invest in it, and grow it. If not, we develop another one, because options and opportunities are appearing all the time if you listen hard enough. I believe that, as a leader, you must open yourself up to ideas and arguments that you might at first find difficult, because, in doing so, you get better ones.'*

Profoundly deaf since birth, Genevieve Barr has forged a successful career both as a young actress and with Common Purpose. She explains the value of turbulent networks in persuading doubters and overcoming resistance: '*I have watched leaders finding a person who is going to disagree with their ideas, and encouraging feedback from them. This way, they find out about all the potential snags. And then, by going back to the person time and time again, they fine-tune the idea until it's beyond the path of resistance. This approach trains you to welcome all responses: and it means that you anticipate every potential negative response. It requires the leader to have turbulent networks, people who can help to apply ideas to different contexts and cultures. I do it myself now. In the disabled world, everyone has a different issue or obstacle which means that you have to find multiple means for one simple thing to work. You don't necessarily have to change the idea: but you often have to change the means and how you communicate it, after you have used your networks to test and refine it.*'

I have a friend who is Head of Risk at a large international bank. He expands the network idea from the group to the individual: '*A turbulent network is crucial, full of people who read different things from you, and watch the stuff you don't watch. People who are ideologically opposed to you. They will keep you out of dangerous comfort. But, on reflection, maybe it's not turbulent networks you need, but turbulent relationships. Ones that are strong, but uncomfortable. I think you have to consciously look out for them and treasure them. If you get a call from someone who makes your blood boil, take it. If you get a paper from them which you want to tear up, read it again. Don't buy, go, recruit or sell without listening to them.*'

Essential though such networks are, I do not underestimate the difficulty of creating them. Generally, and not surprisingly, human beings much prefer support networks. We all seek out people like ourselves. You see it the world over, and throughout history. Pick pretty much any organisation of human beings, anywhere, and you will see the same tendency to 'like people like you', and form networks that exclude, however subtly, people who are different. People who then form their own networks that are largely designed to do the same. So I went to South Africa, where the divides have been most dramatically bridged, and I spoke to two people from the generation who must surely be its biggest beneficiaries.

Firstly, I talked to Dalisu Jwara, an undergraduate student at the University of Cape Town. He was brought up by his grandmother in a township after both his parents died of AIDS when he was five, and he had struggled all his life to get to university. We discussed the fact that, having recruited students from many different backgrounds, so many universities then seem doomed to watch them congregate around their own types. He said that when he arrived at UCT his heart leapt: he thought he had *'finally found Mandela's Rainbow Nation'*. But, after some time, he realised the truth. Rich white students stick to themselves, poor white students to themselves, rich black students to themselves and poor black students to themselves. Hindu Indians and Muslim Indians operate separately, and Cape Malays stick with Cape Malays. His list was exhaustive as he went through all the separate groups, one by one. 'And they don't mix?' I asked. *'They just don't,'* he replied. *'There are a few like me who buck the trend, but not many.'* I asked about sport: doesn't that encourage blurring of these boundaries? *'Yes, that has some mixing effect,'* he replied. *'But the big sports are cricket and rugby: and they are white sports.'*

The next day, I spoke to Khadija Rhoda, a student in Johannesburg who would describe herself as Cape Malay. Surely it must be different there? *'No, it is the same. As a young person – having not lived as an adult under apartheid – it is hard when you slowly realise that it is gone in substance, but not in spirit. Eradicating it will take many generations, which is not what you want to admit when you are young. Apartheid threw everyone who was not white together, including my family. But, rather than unite – against a common white enemy – we just split up into new hierarchies. Apartheid sort of made everyone want to be better than someone else. Even if you hated it, your self-image was built on being superior to someone. And now, at university, I see all those old hierarchies are still there. White, coloured, Indian, black – and then there are all the layers in between. At university, you have to add all the groupings of students from other countries who congregate around each other as well. And here, they don't just congregate: in South Africa, we make sure that there is also a pecking order, and it develops fast.'*

Both these young people know that they live in a time, and in a country, where the opportunity to bridge the traditional divides is huge, where they are surrounded by people with whom they can build diverse networks. For many of us, there is no better place to start the journey to CQ than a university full of people from different backgrounds and different countries. Yet, even in South Africa, they are struggling to compete with the forces of fragmentation that drag people apart and to 'the same', rather than coming together and experiencing 'different'. This story repeats itself in universities across the world.

After university, of course, they will find it even harder, as they enter organisations with long histories of 'us and them', full of their own factions and pecking orders; where many people survive perfectly happily building up collections of business cards, rather than creating the real relationships that are required to solve bigger and more complicated problems, and without realising that, in large parts of the world, you will need these relationships to make things happen.

I discussed this with Carlos Arruda, Executive Director of International Partnerships at Fundação Dom Cabral, the leading Brazilian Business School. He confirmed the distinction: *'Brazilian society is built on relationships. Leaders without networks don't succeed. In Brazil, we say "to do business together, we must eat a bag of salt". In other words, it takes a long, long time. And, if the relationship is at risk, then the decision will get delayed. Relationships are more important than results. They are for life in Brazil.'*

This is also the case in India, and China, and Africa. There is a widespread view that the Internet will save the day, putting us all in touch with pretty much anyone we want to reach, with the technology to open discussions and forge relationships that were inconceivable even a decade ago. Of course, it has that potential. But, for some, there is a huge temptation to use the Internet to create new forms of closed clubs. To seek out yet more 'people like me', who just happen to be further away.

I believe that this temptation simply to increase one's homogeneous networks needs to be resisted. In order to address complex problems and bring people together to solve them, leaders have to go further afield, and further away from what (and who) they know. They will need to build turbulent networks that will challenge and discomfit them. That will take more than a good Internet connection. It will require CQ.

The importance of trust

In this new, less structured world, trust will become the greatest of assets. People buy brands they trust, listen to sources they trust and choose to follow leaders they trust. Without that trust, they will not give of their best. Or worse, they will eventually simply move on to someone they do trust. There's an old saying in the advertising business

– you can tell people you're funny, or you can make them laugh. It's like that with trust, I think.

Venture philanthropist Peter Kulloi in Budapest highlights the importance of trust as a personal asset: '*I see myself as a brand. And I live in a region of the world which is very corrupt, where the state is not there to serve the people, but to exercise power, and they have a lot of it. I have tried to keep out of this. I suppose I value freedom more than anything else. My brand is probably my greatest asset, and I hope it is associated with trust.*'

It's hard to disagree with this. Maintaining your personal brand is a crucial element of building trust. But I think you have to go one step further.

Baroness Onora O'Neill is a philosopher, a crossbench member of the House of Lords and Chair of the Equality and Human Rights Commission in the UK. When I discussed trust with her, she put a completely different emphasis on it: '*If I am the leader, the onus should not be on you to trust me. It is up to me to make myself worthy of your trust. The important word is not trust: it's trustworthy. Trustworthiness is what we are aiming for.*' As a word, it's a bit of a mouthful, but she's right, I think. It is up to the leader to take action: to make good decisions, to behave consistently and appropriately, and to build up a record of this over time. That's the way to become, and remain, worthy of people's trust.

It's one thing doing this in your own culture or sector, where the reference points for trust will be familiar on all sides. It is much harder to establish your own trustworthiness with people whose frame of reference for trust is very different. Here is a simple example. In my own culture, one of the things I naturally do to establish my own trustworthiness is to look people straight in the eye. This is natural to me, and seems well established across Western culture, but it is not the same everywhere. Issa Baluch told me a revealing story of a clash on this issue: '*My oldest friend – we were classmates together in Africa – went to live in Canada. And for the first three years, he could not get a job. He was well brought up so, if anyone older than him looked him in the eyes, he would look down to show respect. He had many interviews, but never got appointed. It seems that they thought he had too much pride, or was stupid, or even lacked integrity. In the end, the headhunter who had been putting him forward figured out what was going wrong and told him that, if he did not look people in the eyes in Canada, no one would trust him or appoint him.*'

But we also have to recognise that, in some cultures, the same action has the opposite effect. It destroys trustworthiness. When you start to work with people from other cultures, you also have to decide who you are going to trust. To continue the example: if my trust reference point is eye contact and no one will look me in the eye, how do I decide who to trust?

There is much more to this than gestures or local customs. If you're used to working with men and you know how to assess who you can trust, how do you go about recruiting women? If you're French and your antennae naturally tell you which French people to trust, how do you operate in China? If you know who to trust in the private sector because you know how they think, how do you assess who to trust in the public sector? If you trust the instincts of people in your own generation, how do you judge the instincts of people who are younger or older? The answer to all these questions is CQ.

The demands of demographics

Relationships between old and young are becoming increasingly strained, right across the world. In some cases, it is through a decline in young people who are then feeling the strain of looking after their elders. In other cases, it is because of an abundance of young, who want things to be different and are not prepared to wait. Leaders with CQ – young and old – will need to cross the generations.

Perhaps it is a natural precondition of progress that young and old must clash. But I believe it is also a precondition of progress that they must connect. I have heard many times, all over the world, variations on 'Oh, they won't be interested in an old man like me' (the old man sometimes being in his forties). Or, from a young person, 'They don't want to hear the youth voice'. The more these words are uttered, the more self-fulfilling they become.

Why, if you go to supper with friends, do they so often have younger people at the other end of the table? Or on another table, or even in another room? Adults justify it on the basis that 'we are old and boring, and they won't be interested in us'. Well, they won't if we never speak to each other.

Sir Eric Thomas agrees: '*I just don't understand why people will not resist the temptation to go on about "the youth of today". They moan that the young are not like we were: yet evolution and genetics guarantee that they are. I once tried to research the oldest use of the phrase. I think it was Nestor, an ancient Greek warrior in the* Iliad, *in 600BC. And we have gone on about it, generation after generation, ever since.*'

Generations seem doomed to stray apart, muttering about each other, when what they should do is see the world through each other's eyes and talk to each other. I believe this is true everywhere, but there are places where the problem is particularly pressing.

Alyque Padamsee is a highly experienced actor, theatre producer and film maker in India. He tells me: '*India is the youngest large nation in the world. Fifty per cent of the population is under 25 years old, while 50 per cent of the top leaders are over 70 years old.*'

Issa Baluch sees the same thing, in a different part of the world: '*In Africa and the Middle East, families say very little to each other. An enormous amount is taken for granted. I myself think that if you work with young people you stay young at heart and your life is constantly renewed. That's why I decided not to play golf every day, but to go to Harvard.*'

Given the starkness of the demographics now, I find the lost opportunity all this represents deeply frustrating.

Increasingly, I attend meetings and events on the impact of shifting demographics. At these events, I invariably hear established leaders talking about 'harnessing young people'. They seem to forget just what harnesses are: thick pieces of leather that are strapped around an animal's head to make it go faster, to force it to go where it doesn't want to go, or to hold it back and slow it down.

My instinct says that the established leaders who will succeed will do exactly the opposite to all this 'harnessing'. They will be the ones young people will choose to follow, choose to learn from and choose to throw their energies and ideas behind. But it will require the leaders to accept the different cultures of different generations; to resist the temptation to preach or use excessive control; to allow others to 'have it easier than we did'; and to engage and support the young leaders emerging around them.

It also calls for young leaders who will cross the generational divides and boundaries and who will grab the benefits of working with established leaders and will steal from them their knowledge and experience. Taking what is good and – I hope – discarding what is not, playing with everything in between. Going one step further on the great ideas, and adapting the ones that haven't worked yet, but could. I believe that these young leaders will jump ahead as they avoid dismissing established leaders, or putting them on a pedestal (which we will all inevitably fall off at some point), or paying them necessary homage but with their ears firmly shut.

Martin Kalungu-Banda is a Zambian who acts as an adviser to numerous governments in Africa. He gave me a vivid example of the challenge: '*In Africa, age is what you respect. Failing to pay that respect will write you off as a leader. The respect can come in many forms. It can be deep affection and eager open ears, seeking to learn and pass on every possible piece of wisdom. Or it can be blind, unquestioning respect which is polite, but not a learning experience. Or it can be the illusion of deep respect which is a sham again, because no learning is exchanged.*'

Recently, I came across a company with a different approach to the generation issue. Young leaders were asked to mentor older leaders, the task being to get young leaders to remind older leaders what it was like to be young. I am told that the conversations that emerged were quite wonderful: they built up CQ in both generations as they worked side by side as equals, and transformed the culture of the whole organisation.

The spark of innovation

Everywhere you look, everyone is crying out for innovation: new ways, new ideas, new processes, new technologies, new ventures. I believe that the secret of innovation is that it comes best from well-led discord. The enemy is 'group-think'. Mixed groups – led by leaders with CQ – see things differently. They help each other to think the unthinkable. They take ideas and turn them on their heads, and, in the process, they break out of 'group-think' – to create something genuinely new.

In East and West alike, there are calls for 'frugal innovation'. In the developed world, because we have to achieve more with less; and in the developing world, because we have to reach more and more people. Einstein defined insanity as 'doing the same thing over and over again and expecting different results'. I believe that innovation will not come from working with people who think like you do, or who operate in the same way, or in the same space.

Some years ago, when I was running Common Purpose in the UK, I got a last-minute invitation to a meeting on gun crime in London the following day. It was not an email but a phone call, so it was harder to say no. What I did say was, 'but I know nothing about gun crime'. I was then told that that was exactly why he wanted me: the session was to be a brainstorm to look at new ways to deal with the problem. So I went the next day to a very swanky building, and was sent up to a very swanky room. As I walked in, I realised that the entire room was full of policemen and policewomen. I respect police officers, but the thought that you could spend four hours in a meeting looking for new ways to address gun crime with members of the police force alone was, to me, utterly ridiculous. It would need people from housing and health, from education and transport, bankers and lawyers, community workers and street cleaners – not to mention politicians and probation officers. For once (I don't usually have the courage), I left quietly at midday. Group-think was setting in, and there was just no prospect of shifting it.

Solutions – genuinely innovative ones – don't come from homogeneity, they come from combining differences. People saying different things, speaking from opposite points of view; arguing the unarguable; playing with crazy ideas; questioning, challenging – sometimes even offending – one another; prodding and prompting ourselves to shift our thinking and play with really different ideas. This process seldom works if it's led by people who are so frightened of dissonance and discord – and of saying the wrong thing – that they rush to close it all down. It calls for leaders with CQ. Leaders who are not frightened by difference and conflict; who don't think it's polite to ignore difference or pretend it isn't there; who are not timid about having dissonance in the room, and giving it its place. Leaders who don't want to 'iron out the differences' – quite the opposite.

Alan Rosling is the former Director of Tata Sons and now co-founder of Kiran Energy in India. He actively looks for people like this: '*Innovation comes from difference. Today, I look at boards to see how one-dimensional they are. This has nothing to do with justice, or principle, or "diversity". I am just assessing whether they are likely to be innovators or not. Some boards in India have people who are all from the same state, and who even went to school with each other.*'

Innovation needs people who actively seek to encourage difference. To prod it, push it, test it, enjoy it and thrive on it. People who want to de-harness – even if they secretly know that they have no real idea where it might take them, just that it won't be where they went before.

The urban magnet

People are moving around the world as never before, and this will only accelerate as climate change dictates the areas of the world where people can live. People all over the world are urbanising: gravitating to cities and away from rural communities. There are now 30 cities in India with over 1 million inhabitants. In China, there are now 160, and worldwide, there are now 31 cities with populations of more than 10 million, from Lagos to Tehran, from Karachi to Guangzhou.

Some of these cities are not just growing in size; they are (or are fast becoming) magnets of talent, all coming together from multiple countries and different cultures. I believe that there are now about 200 cities around the world that have this 'magnet' status. The obvious ones are London, Hong Kong and New York, as they always have been. But many other cities are coming up fast alongside them. To be a leader in any of these cities, people will need to have serious CQ. They will need to be able to set diverse groups alight, and not set out to homogenise them, instructing them to leave their difference at the door. They will need to create a culture that allows people to belong while being different, and to be many different things all at the same time.

These cities will thrive only if they have enough leaders with CQ in every sector: public, private and NGO, and from every generation. Alan

Lau, the Senior Assistant Commissioner of the Hong Kong Police Force, sees this very clearly: *'CQ is essential in cities like mine, where everyone has different backgrounds, education and economic circumstances. We have always received new groups: mainland Chinese, European, Indian, Pakistani, Nepalese and African. Some are now second- and even third-generation Hong Kong citizens. They all want to achieve and make things happen. Policing them by knowing the systems and protocols only would be a waste of time. You have to develop an understanding of the different cultures, to have conversations which are only about building relationships, to show that you are interested and hear them, and when you can, you will act on it. This is how you bring people together. If you are policing a city like Hong Kong, you often have to motivate people to do things they need to do but don't want to do.*

Maybe it's even more needed in Hong Kong because, since 1997, we have had to make two very different systems and cultures work alongside each other – and there was no precedent of its kind. We have had to build it by talking about difficult stuff and drawing difficult and sometimes unwelcome lines. During this time, we have shifted the entire culture of the police from almost a paramilitary force to a values-based one. In the 70s, we "fought" crime, and corruption was a huge problem. Today, we have had to earn the mandate to police the city.'

I think this highlights something else that is true of the world's magnet cities: their citizens delight in the fact that they are 'hybrids', with multiple backgrounds and identities. For them, the 'mixed blood' of Ron Arculli's childhood is no longer a weakness; it's a source of strength.

Forty years younger than Ron, Riz Ahmed is a London-born actor and rapper, of Pakistani heritage. When I spoke to him, he was working in New York: *'I grew up between classes and races. I had a mongrelised hybrid upbringing. I am almost trapped in chameleonism, and I love it. It's my strength, my USP, my asset.'*

Leaders in such cities who ask the question 'Where are you from?' and expect a one-word answer (and glaze over when they get more than one) risk making themselves irrelevant.

Amali de Alwis is a young Thought Leadership Consultant currently on secondment at the World Economic Forum. She loves asking this question, not for the one-word answer, but because it opens up a discussion:

'I love seeing where people take the question to. What they refer to. Their parents, their heritage, their geography, their schools, their jobs. It tells me so much.'

Another key definition of magnet cities is that they attract students. Indeed, it is estimated that the number of students who will travel to another country to study will double from its figure of 3.7 million in 2009 to over 7 million by 2020.[1] To be a student in such a city, where vast numbers of people of hundreds of different nationalities congregate, is an incredible opportunity to learn CQ. As Dalisu and Khadija say, this is not happening in South Africa, and I have a feeling that the same is true the world over. I am told that, if mainland Chinese students come to the UK to study, their English language skills will have gone down by the end of their first year, through talking endlessly with other mainland Chinese students. In keeping to themselves, they lose the opportunity to develop CQ, in cities that are built for it. It is not just students who will lose this opportunity. In vibrant, growing cities such as this, any leader who does not have CQ will simply be left out.

Growing world, shrinking leaders

The number of people with global roles is multiplying. They travel almost constantly and they touch down frequently: sometimes for a day, a week, a month, a quarter or a year. They are expected to deliver wherever they land, and deliver fast. This will call for ever more CQ.

My father was, in many ways, at the forefront of globalisation. He was from Manchester, and his two business partners were a Jew brought up in the Christian quarter of Baghdad and an Iranian, based in Washington. We lived in London, New York and then Geneva: all places where everyone had multiple roots and very different stories to tell; where the unusual people were the homogeneous ones.

He spent a lot of time travelling, doing deals around the world, and he saw more and more leaders starting to join him on the planes. He used to call them the 'Flying Dead'. People who described themselves – in an increasingly haughty fashion – as 'global'. People who would fly around the world, stop every now and then and be expected to deliver, with no real idea where they were (and, increasingly, who they were). His fear was that the Flying Dead would end up running the world, simply because they travelled it.

Globalisation has meant that there are more potential Flying Dead leaders than ever before. They are a strange breed. Many, of course, would claim to have CQ in abundance. Unfortunately, they measure it in Air Miles. The real challenge for them is to get enough CQ so that, when they land, they understand where they are and who they're talking to, and then use what they have learned to succeed.

In my view, the leaders who fail to do this will just continue collecting stamps on their passports without really touching down anywhere they land, while the ones who do it well will become bridge-builders who can genuinely change the world.

The pressure to focus

I have always thought that the leadership journey looks very much like an hourglass. As your career progresses, you become more and more knowledgeable in a smaller and smaller field. And then, suddenly, you get that next promotion when you need a broader view again and nothing has prepared you for it. This is one of the reasons we began Common Purpose back in 1989. I think the forces that create the narrowing of the lens are even stronger now than they were then.

It is not altogether surprising, given the shock the world has undergone since 2010, when the credibility of leadership itself has been seriously questioned, at every level and in all sectors. History shows that leaders (and people in general) react to such shocks by looking inwards and building new walls.

But when dangers and pitfalls – and opportunities – surround you, it is the job of a leader to spot them and, ideally, anticipate them, because they can come from unexpected places and in unexpected ways. That demands a wider lens – at the very point when everything and everyone else is pressing you to focus. I remember that, all through my education and early career, people kept telling me to be focused. Focus,

focus, focus: whether it was passing exams or securing promotions. Leaders who are focused get on, everyone said, but I think there is a problem with this myth, because leaders who are too focused can be very dangerous, especially if the focus is entirely at the price of seeing the wider context.

Much of my leadership learning seems to involve boats. I hate boats – especially sailing, so maybe the learning comes less from the sailing itself and more from doing something that is not natural to me and so I do it badly. Three summers ago, I decided that my kids were old enough to sail without me and that my presence in the boat was no longer required, so I could, instead, walk along the cliff to where we were due to meet for lunch. From the cliff path, I watched them weave and tilt in a way they never would have done with a nervous me in the boat. Then they turned – and the boat flipped over. All you could see was the bottom of the boat, facing upwards out of the water. There was an unlucky couple on the cliff path. I ran over, ripped the man's binoculars off his neck and trained them on the upturned boat. I counted the heads as they appeared – desperately slowly, and I watched the older ones heave the younger ones out of the freezing Scottish water and on to the upturned keel. My eyes were glued to them, my heart was racing and my head was going mad, because I knew I could do nothing to help them. My mind was fixated on counting and recounting to check that no one had slipped off again. My ears were shut and my eyes were fixed to the narrow binocular lenses. I never saw how beautiful the sea was, nor the weather, nor the blue-purple islands across the sparkling sea to Jura, all of which might have calmed me down. I never saw the coast-guard's boat, crossing the sea at speed. All I saw was their heads, and their grim attempts to get more of them out of the sea and on to the capsized boat. Looking back now, my blindness and deafness were quite extraordinary. One look up, and I would have seen the context and known that all would be well.

Over the last two years at Common Purpose, watching so many companies and charities go under in the economic turmoil, I have often felt that I was back on that cliff. Not as a mother, but as a leader (and founder) of Common Purpose. All the sea analogies work: storm clouds, choppy seas, tall unwelcoming cliffs to fall off or crash against and limited supplies (we have always concentrated on growth at Common

Purpose, and never just built up reserves). And the truth is that, if we had become too focused and narrowed our vision only on survival, we would have missed some enormous opportunities that have come our way, even with the storm raging about us.

Instead, we looked up and we grasped them. We grew our student work fivefold. We opened new operations in Asia Pacific and South America. We launched the Study Conference for Commonwealth Leaders (CSCLeaders) in partnership with the Duke of Edinburgh Commonwealth Study Conference. We went to Libya – funded by the EU – to run courses for leaders in Benghazi, Tripoli, Misrata and Derna, and much more.

If my eyes – or those of my colleagues and our Board – had stayed glued to the binoculars, none of this would have happened. Mothers and fathers might be forgiven for being too focused, but leaders will never be.

I told this story a couple of years ago when I was giving a speech in Tripoli. A man in the audience told me: 'You know, that's often why war photographers die first. They have their eyes glued to the camera lens – with its narrow field of vision, even if it is wide-angle – and they don't see what is coming from either side, or above or below them.'

If you don't see context, you don't see what is coming. Whether it's a problem, or a blow, or a way through, or a golden opportunity. I believe that the legitimacy of a leader comes partly from the fact that he or she does see the wider picture. I would go as far as to say that if you don't – or can't – then that is the moment to walk away and leave it to a leader who can. You owe this to your colleagues, and to the task at hand.

Based in India, Alan Rosling advises ambitious young leaders, in Asia Pacific especially, to get out of the office: 'They work very long hours, and they're very focused on the task. The effect is that they miss walking in the streets, hearing what is happening and seeing what people are thinking.'

Adam Habib in South Africa agrees: 'You have to see context as a leader, or you are doomed to making endless bad decisions. Take our Education Act. It was totally admirable, but it didn't work, because it lacked context. It relied on parents helping their children with homework, but very few parents in South Africa are educated enough to help. And, even if they are, they don't have enough *electricity to allow the kids to study at night. Another example: South African students don't do postgraduate degrees, so we launched lots of scholarships. But if you are poor and your parents have saved and suffered for your education, when you get money for postgrad, you will give it to your parents.'*

Jim Sutcliffe is Managing Partner at Arboretum Partners LLP and Chairman of Sun Life Financial in Canada. He stresses the business value of CQ in helping managers to see the wider context in which the company operates: *'You need CQ to run a business today, because, in the long run, you will make more money with CQ. I know we have all thought business was about products, customers, finances and people, but it's more than that now. You have to understand the context in which you are operating and the communities you are part of. You have to work with other sectors and, if you are international, in other countries, and you need it not just at the top, but right through the business. Without it, you won't judge when to stand firm and when to give way, when to spend money, whether you like it or not. Without it, you will walk into impossible, messy situations that are sometimes at least partly of your own making. And, when the solutions do not lie in financial models, better products or new technologies, you will make bad judgements, because none of those things are much use when you are dealing with the media and politics, and you find yourself and your company in the public eye.'*

This calibration of focus and context has been a long battle for me, at work and at home. At work, I want everyone at Common Purpose to have at least one work meeting in their diary every month which they could not possibly justify as directly relevant to or focused on their current workload. One meeting a month on context seems like a baseline requirement to keep focus and context in balance. Once, years ago now, I came home from work one day to find a note on the hall table from my daughter Rachel's headmistress. Rachel was eight at the time, and the note said that she 'lacked focus'. I sent a note back. It read: 'At the age of eight, I think this a jolly good thing.' And not just at eight. Focus is good, context is better, and you'll need CQ to strike the right balance.

So there are my eight reasons why CQ has found its time, and leaders need to develop it and develop it soon. Now the question moves on: from why to how.

Scenario: Past, present, future: how influential are they?

My father used to ask leaders he met around the world one question: *'What influences your decisions the most: the past, the present or the future?'* Then he would ask them to draw a different circle for each one, with the size of the circle indicating the strength of the influence for them. I can see him now, leaning across a dinner table, having found a folded piece of paper in his pocket (and, failing that, a paper napkin), getting the person to draw their circles for him. He never let them think for long. He was interested in their first responses.

Over the last few months, while I have been writing this book, I have copied his idea, and, as the people I spoke to drew their circles, I have captured some of the things they said to explain them. Here are just a few of them:

A Russian businessman

The past: *'The past guides everything, and it was violent.'*

The present: He had nothing much to say on the present.

The future: *'Because, you must understand, it may never happen.'*

A mainland Chinese corporate leader

The past: *'It doesn't matter: because we can't change it.'*

The present: *'Though it is only a connector: a connector to build on.'*

The future: *'Everything is about the future because China thinks long term.'*

An academic in Brazil

The past: *'The past is simply not relevant. If we looked at the past, we would be frozen, because of the stop-start nature of Brazil. We have an expression here: "the cat that was shocked by cold water never goes near water again".'*

The present: *'This time, we must demonstrate continuous progress towards the future.'*

The future: *'In Brazil, as leaders, we are full of hope.'*

A hospital Director in Turkey

The past: *'We have to learn from our past.'*

The present: *'We are making the best of the present.'*

The future: *'Who knows. I can't even book a summer holiday.'*

A policeman in Asia-Pacific

The past: *'As time goes by, the past becomes smaller and smaller in our minds as it is less and less relevant.'*

The present: *'The present has dominated ever since 1997 because, as leaders of Hong Kong, we know that we have to make some very hard and good decisions now if the future is to be bright.'*

The future: *'And it will be huge, if we get the present right.'*

A business leader in Germany

The past: *'The past is fragmented in Germany, and recent history is so awful that it can dominate your thinking.'*

The present: *'We are developing confidence and getting better at putting the past behind us but we are still unsure of ourselves.'*

The future: *'We are holding our own economically, even punching above our weight.'*

A retired US ambassador

The past: *'We really do take the past for granted.'*

The present: *'It is the overwhelming influencing factor.'*

The future: *'I think we really don't think much about the future; again, we take it for granted that we will figure it out.'*

An Arab government leader from the Gulf

The past: *'History has not been kind to us, so we try not to think about it.'*

The present: *'Like the Russian businessman, he skipped over the present.'*

The future: *'It is enormous, mainly because there is just so much to be done.'*

You can do a variant of the exercise if you have people of different ages at the table:

A senior NGO leader in India

The past: *'We have a rich heritage. Indian leaders think we must live up to the superheroes of the past: the leaders who created the Indian state and led the great Indian companies, the Ambanis and the Tatas, and great men like Gandhi, Bhagat Singh, Nehru, Bal Gangadhar Tilak, Subhas Chandra Bose. We make our decisions in their shadows.'*

The present: *'The present is only a bridge between the past and the future. Other than that, it just doesn't matter.'*

The future: *'Leaders in India think of the unknown as exactly that: the unknown. So they do not factor it into their decisions much.'*

The young student sitting next to him in Mumbai

He agreed – but only on the present. His circles looked like this:

The past: *'It's full of old resentments which I feel people are moving on from.'*

The present: *'We have to act now, urgently.'*

The future: *'Because we have everything to go for in this amazing country.'*

And here is another variant, which looks at the issue from the viewpoints of people in different sectors:

A West African business leader

I asked him whether the situation looks different in different sectors. He only sees variations in the past and the future: *'I think some leaders in the private sector look to the past because they remember a time when things were easier – when palms could be greased. But for most people in the private sector, the future is a big circle full of African opportunities.'* He thought it was probably a bit different for the NGO and public sectors: *'They are very eager to move on from the past, but they are consumed by the present in a way that makes the future quite a small circle.'*

If this is West Africa, how does it look further south?

A bishop in Southern Africa

The past: *'Too many still blame the present on the past, and this poisons us.'*

The present: *'It's the dynamic place where the past and present connect.'*

The future: *'We remain very trusting and hopeful that the next leaders will be better.'*

It's a revealing process, I think. Try it next time you are with leaders from different cultures (but keep spare pieces of paper in your pocket – the napkins can get very messy).

---

1. Altbach, Philip G., Liz Reisberg and Laura E. Rumbley. *Trends in Global Higher Education: Tracking an Academic Revolution*. Paris: United Nations Educational, Scientific and Cultural Organisation, 2009.

Part Three

Developing your CQ: Core and Flex

The process of developing the CQ that will enable you go out and thrive in different cultures starts by looking inwards, at yourself. In particular, at two aspects of yourself. I call them 'Core' and 'Flex'. Both help to define you as a leader, although they are quite different.

Your 'Core' comprises the things that you believe define you: your own personal 'over my dead body' list. These are things that won't change (or won't change easily). Their solidity is your strength.

In your 'Flex' are things that will change. Things that will adapt to circumstances, or to other people or other cultures. Their fluidity is equally your strength. This section of the book explores them and how (and when, and why) they might change.

A constant review

So the starting point is to ask yourself (and keep asking) what is your Core and what is your Flex? A lot of CQ comes through unpicking these two and getting the balance more or less right, and keeping the line between your Core and Flex under constant review as you grow older, as you experience new things and as the world changes around you.

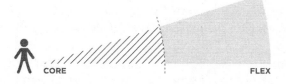

More than 'values'

In both Core and Flex you'll find a combination of many things. Values are in there, for sure. The trouble is that the expression 'core values' trips too easily off the tongue for most leaders nowadays, as they dust off their organisation's mission statement, or dig out the slides they prepared earlier. We know that the word 'integrity' will feature on at least one of them, so we just ignore it when it comes up on the screen. It has lost its meaning and its power, which is why, as a word, 'values' has lost so much of its real value. In any case, I think it's more complicated than a list of values.

I realised how much I was messing things up when I talked to a big player in the diversity field in South Africa. She talked me through the coaching hierarchy she uses to help leaders to become clearer about their purpose. Her approach is informed by Robert Dilts's Logical Levels, which is based on the understanding that higher order values and beliefs (such as spirituality and identity) inform and influence lower level beliefs, values and behaviours. As I spoke about CQ and the Core she said: 'Yes, of course. You are talking about the top layers: Identity and the Spirit.'

But, on reflection, I'm not sure that's right. I don't think Core sits at the top, as a higher order, with Flex somewhere beneath it. I think Core and Flex run through every one of her levels, from top to bottom. In Core, for example, lies everything from Spirit and Identity to Behaviours and Environment. Whether my Behaviours embody my Beliefs and Identity or not, to other people (and particularly people from other cultures), how I behave is a pretty crucial external manifestation. And I might find it difficult to move some of these Behaviours from my Core.

Here's a very personal example (since it's hard to discuss Core and Flex without drawing on the personal). I have always been very tactile. As a child, I found it very difficult to use cutlery; I always wanted to feel my food, or squeeze it between my fingers. Since I can remember, I have found it almost impossible not to touch people. I often kiss them on each cheek as we meet or part; at the very least, I shake their hand with conviction, even sometimes with my other hand cupping their elbow. I like to pat people gently on the back when they have done something wonderful or, even more importantly, stroke their back when they need encouragement and support.

Even after 30 years, I hold hands with my husband at every possible opportunity, and I know that we look utterly ridiculous when we go for walks or arrive at fancy events hand in hand. As we arrived at one recently, a friend said, *'You'll never be a power couple if you insist on holding hands'*. I am sure that this tactile behaviour is so established and deep-rooted – and so incredibly difficult to drop – that it has belonged in my Core for many, many years. It's me, it's what I do, and I do it instinctively, almost unconsciously.

But now I have started working in countries and societies where, as a woman in particular, I can't do it. (Though it's important to say there are very few places where it really is an absolute no-no.) So, with huge pain and discomfort and unease, I have managed – on rare occasions – to shift this tactile behaviour from my Core to my Flex.

With most people, I proceed as normal, and I must admit that I sometimes forget – genuinely forget. I gave an imam a huge kiss when I saw him last year. You should never kiss an imam. I gave him a kiss (actually two, one on each cheek, like I always do) because he is a wonderful man, because I was so delighted to see him after some time and because I was thinking about who he is, not what he is. He smiled, looked down and shuffled. Months later – when quizzed about it by a fellow imam who had witnessed the incident – he explained that 'it was just Julia'. He is a lovely man whom I have promised never to kiss again. And, although I did it for the best of reasons, I was in the wrong.

Enough Core

Leaders need to know what is in their Core, because if they are not aware of it – both the good and the bad – they will confuse and unsettle themselves, and others, on a regular basis.

Dr Reuel Khoza is Non-Executive Chairman of Nedbank in Johannesburg. I asked him how he defines his Core: *'Which bits of my Core do I cherish? Honesty, probity and accountability. I don't tell a lie with ease. I am too transparent: my daughters say that my face is very round, and it gets even more round if I try to lie. I have always hated that expression "a white lie". It's a lie that people believe to be harmless, as no one will ostensibly suffer. No it's not a good expression. I also have a deep work ethic. My grandfather said: "You may not rest unless you are tired". You have to push yourself: "If you rest and you are not tired, you are indolent". My grandfather said this to many of his grandchildren and it affected us all differently. For me, it is unchangeable. Even now, when I have an option to rest early, I work long hard hours each day.'*

As you start to unpick your Core and test it, I think you hit two hurdles – and one dead end. The first hurdle is that you discover all the things you thought were Core that don't quite pass when you put them to the test. The second hurdle is that you uncover the things that you realise could be bias (whether conscious or not) that you will have to probe and test further. And the dead end? Things you are ashamed of but can't shift from your Core and can only compensate for.

For me, the best example of Core that might actually be Flex has come through parenting (times five, in my case), which certainly shifted my Core inwards and left me with a great deal more Flex than I thought I originally had.

In the early baby days, exhausted through lack of sleep, I found myself constantly having to distinguish between what I believed really mattered from all the kind advice on hand: the relentless voices of caution, the surprising pressures exerted, the strange traditions built up over the years and the unending instructions given. An example? Whether to leave your baby to cry him or herself to sleep. Do you realise that if you leave babies to cry, you could be failing to prepare them for the hard real world and mollycoddling them from the start to be weak and wet? 'It's a tough world,' they all told me. 'She has to understand this from the start.' To me, this was utterly nonsensical. Yet it was said by people with huge experience, whose advice on most matters I would previously have taken with no hesitation. It was an issue that I found easy to sort: because it was right at the heart of my Core. There was no possible room for Flex. I could never leave a baby to cry – and I ignored the lot of them. (No doubt producing thoroughly pathetic, spoilt children, who all know I will always be there for them.)

Then, as they grew and started to speak, it became tougher to align my husband's and my – not identical but mostly compatible – Cores on things such as education and discipline. And then came the even more demanding early teenage years, in which I found myself in situations I had never dreamt of being in and made a fool of myself by taking a position on an issue which, in truth, I had only taken in the heat of the moment.

In those days, I discovered things about myself that surprised me – and the kids too, mostly in situations which sprang up suddenly and produced an instant response. Now that my children are adults, I have realised that they each have slightly different Cores, different both from mine and from each other's, so this calls for yet another review.

The point is that even the most solid Cores adapt, to changing circum-stances and over time. So maybe the line between Core and Flex isn't a line at all, but rather a sliding scale that moves very cautiously and slowly, but is capable of sliding nonetheless.

Biases are more frightening. As my father used to say: *'Don't believe anyone who claims not to hold biases. They are either lying to you or to them-selves.'* And he didn't stop there. *'And those of us who have experienced prejudice? We are the worst. Sometimes, we think it makes us experts in preju-dice, and therefore beyond holding biases ourselves. But you can suffer from prejudice because you are gay, and yet still be sexist yourself. You can be deaf and struggling with all the assumptions around deafness, and yet still be entirely bigoted about Chinese people.'*

I am tempted to be kinder than that and say that sometimes you just don't recognise your own biases. I have so many; I have slowly had to admit to them, and I try hard to counterbalance them. I fear that there are more to unravel yet, and that, as I get older and more bad-tempered, I could develop more. But, right now, let me confess to just three.

I am biased about people with high IQ. I could argue that this is because I have met too many leaders with high IQ who lack EQ, let alone CQ (and some who even sneer when they are mentioned), but it's probably at least partly because I was a disaster at school. I was always bringing home reports with my bad marks recorded and underlined in red pen, just to make sure that my parents didn't miss them, which they couldn't possibly have done, because there were far too many to miss. So my anti-IQ bias is probably based on my own failure and the envy that results from it. I am also biased about people with upper-class English voices. Why? I loathe the concept that anyone could be born better than anyone else, and, maybe, because my voice is a bit BBC English, and I would hate to be mistaken for British upper class. This bias seems to me to be a perversion of a genuine piece of my Core, which is the belief that all men – and women – are created equal and I translated this unfairly. I suspect there is also a bit of vulnerability in there too (especially when I hear my own voice and realise that I sound exactly like the people I don't want to sound like).

In my mid-twenties, I realised that I was biased about Arabs too: specifically North African Arabs. Having never worked or lived with North African Arabs, I had not noticed my bias against them, but when I did, I found myself taking a step backwards rather than forwards when I met them. I think it was a throwback to my childhood in France (and my French education). It was not conscious – but it was there. As soon as I discovered it, I volunteered to do everything I could with Arabs. I made a lifelong Libyan friend. I joined Arab boards and I worked with Arabs in north London. The bias did not survive the spotlight I put on it.

Since then, I have done my best to sweep the bias away – and to apologise to the people I have been blind to. This summer, I met someone whom I had dismissed outright more than twenty years ago as a result of a totally unsubstantiated opinion of him (and his upper-class accent), which was based on views I had attributed to my Core. Back then, on one occasion I even drove over his foot to avoid him. (Don't ask, it's a long story: let's just say that your prejudices can get you into a real fluster sometimes.) When we met again this year by chance – and he recognised me – I apologised to him and he told me not to, because he had probably deserved it. Such a deeply, frustratingly generous response, from a man I so wanted to be able to dismiss.

Of course, not all the views you have in your Core are based on bias or prejudice. Some are a product of calm judgement, based on a strong and well-aired Core, but they do need to be kept under constant review. They need to face the light and air. They need to be regularly dusted down, examined and tested. Because, for leaders, they produce blind spots, which, at best, means that you miss opportunities and, at worst, means that you fail to hear a voice which could have helped you or you take an extreme position that makes little sense.

As you air this view, you find out exactly what it is. Cultural stuckness, because the view reflects a past from which you haven't moved on? Or cultural ignorance, because you just can't see what's around you? Or have you discovered a dead end: a piece of cultural intolerance that needs to be dealt with? It is necessary either to kick it out altogether or, if you really can't do that, to learn to compensate for it. (We'll come back to that later in the book.) Whatever you discover it is, it's a blind spot. It clouds your judgement, and that limits your CQ.

Over time, you will also find that your Core gets smaller and contains fewer things that really must be there. Shirlene Oh was born in China, and for many years ran a GlaxoSmithKline factory there, which is when I first met her. She is now Vice President of GSK's Sustainable Lab in London. She describes herself like this: '*I have Chinese heritage and I look Chinese, but I am Malaysian by upbringing. I am also a British national, with British children.*' So she has every right to have accumulated quite a big Core. But, in fact, as time has gone on: '*My Core has got smaller. Things I thought were in there I have discovered are not. They melt away, and they're often things I have been holding pretty fast to. I have grown to realise that it is important to have the duality of having core values and, at the same time, the openness to challenge my beliefs and assumptions from experiences of different cultures.*'

But, as it gets smaller, your Core will also become sounder and more robust. And, though this may sound counter-intuitive, the more inflexible your Core becomes over time, the greater your abilities of Flex become, because you'll know where you genuinely can and where you genuinely can't move. All this improves your trustworthiness, and with it, your CQ.

But not too much Core

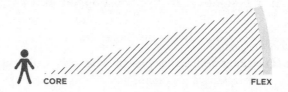

CORE   FLEX

Some leaders are all Core and nothing but Core. They are what they are: 'take me or leave me'. My family's roots are in the North of England: the North as it was in the 1950s, where most sentences started with a sigh, and where 'garlic eaters' were considered to be directly connected with the devil, and almost certainly 'Catholics' (which was about as strange as you could get, and that was pretty bad). Where anyone who didn't laugh at a joke plainly didn't have a sense of humour. I could go on forever. Up north, at that time, their Core was huge and stuffed to capacity. There was no question of any adapting: why would there be? Why adapt, when everyone you know is more or less like you? And if they aren't, at least they have the sense to hide it? My father escaped all this to a job in New York and we discovered a wonderful new world of difference and discord, where no one was like us. Tragically, in the process, we became foreigners to my grandparents, as we discovered that what was now Flex for us remained very much Core for them.

Riz Ahmed agrees: '*You meet so many people who are terrified by the idea of Flex. The world frightens them, so they seek diktats. They don't want to have to think: they want the certainty of orthodoxy. They hang on to their enormous Core for a sense of security – or the illusion of it.*'

There are plenty of leaders today who are 'Core only', with big 'No entry' signs around their necks or on their foreheads. They come in all sectors, from all nationalities and, most depressingly, from all generations (not just grandparents). Sometimes they make a token Flex, to show that they are moving with the times, but it's a thin veneer. For some, it is simply that they are too frightened of the unfamiliar to feel they can Flex on anything. Some are too lazy to bother about other people and see no need to Flex. And a small minority – the truly terrifying – are so convinced of their own rightness that they won't even consider the possibility of Flexing.

Pauline Lafferty is Human Resources Director at the Weir Group plc in Glasgow. I like her take on this: *'Beware people who call themselves citizens of the world: they are citizens of nothing. I often ask myself, did the Scots go out and rule the world but, in ruling it, did they miss an opportunity to understand it?'*

These leaders think that the size and certainty of their Core is their biggest strength. I think it is actually their biggest weakness, because total inflexibility makes CQ completely unattainable.

Enough Flex

So every leader should start with a strong Core and a pretty clear idea of what is in it.

But now we come to Flex. And the first thing I want to stress is that Flex is just as important as Core. Just because it's fluid and adaptable doesn't make it weaker or less valuable. It is quite the opposite. With a strong Core, you can Flex more comfortably, secure in the knowledge that you won't get lost. Reuel Khoza in South Africa put it beautifully: *'As I grew up, my Core anchored me. And the anchor then allowed me to move further. You know that you can float; and the anchor means that you know that you won't float too far.'*

Flexing behaviours

Flex generally starts with behaviours, where you have to get the basics right. Understand the role of shoes and the bottom of the feet in the Arab world. Work out how to eat and greet and dress in different places. Avoid using first names too quickly in much of the world. Know when to bow and when not to bow. Learn when and where to spit because it clears the throat, and where you can't because it disgusts. When to look in the eyes and when to avert them. Where to shake hands and where not to. (The only obvious one I haven't put in this list is smiling, because I haven't yet found anywhere where it's better not to smile. If I'm wrong, please tell me.)

For me, all these behaviours are in Flex, and they're all very important signifiers as you operate in other cultures, not least because they demonstrate that you have Flex and you're not too arrogant (or frightened) to actually Flex it.

As Sir John Parker says: '*You have to show that you can be bothered to learn about other people's cultures. That you can take the time to understand how other people express their values through their behaviour.*' John introduced me to the expression 'behavioural values': how different cultures express their values through different behaviours in different contexts: '*You must bow in Japan; it is how you show deference. At home, I might do this in another way, but, in Japan, I do it their way. You simply have to take account of where you are, and show people that you have done so. You have to get the basics of the Flex right: when to bow, when to smile, how to show that you are polite. This does not mean that you have to change who you are, but it does change how you express it. You have to figure out how other human beings, who have grown up in a different culture and society from you, express their honesty and integrity in their own way, and then you must do it in the same way.*' John summed it up with a strong Irish expression: '*You have to walk towards people.*'

From another generation and the other side of the world, Shirlene Oh agrees. Although, she says, it's getting easier: '*People do get less offended these days. Things have moved on a lot and people are much more culturally sensitive and aware, even over the last ten years. On the whole, people understand social behaviours and etiquette sufficiently, so less offence is taken.*'

I think that the fact that you are less likely to cause irreparable offence does not mean you can ignore the crucial basics of behaviour. There's no quick way to learn it either. There is no course to go on, no graph to pin on the wall, no manual to buy. Born and raised in India, Chris Mathias is a successful international entrepreneur with a very firm view on this: '*There are a lot of people making money peddling the proposition that you can teach it. You can't. You have to learn it. Through experience.*'

If you rely on reading a manual or doing a course, you very quickly get tangled up with someone from somewhere else who has also read a manual or done a course. Recently, I gave a speech on leadership at a business school. A young man in the audience came up to me afterwards. Having been on one of these courses, he wanted to tell me a story: '*They told me that, in China, you should hand over your card with two hands, and bow just a little. Unfortunately, the man I met had been on a course too. He was determined to use only one hand, because I was a Westerner, and to look me in the eyes. So our first meeting was rather messy. We stumbled to exchange our cards – and he almost fell over trying to look at me straight on.*'

We chuckled at the absurdity of thinking that a few behavioural 'tips' can properly prepare you for operating in another culture. They don't, and it's even more important not to seek the simple codifications when you are leading.

Aged 30, Mike Martin has recently left the British Army after six years. A Pushtu speaker, he set up the army's first ever cultural understanding capability, during several tours in Afghanistan: '*I was first asked to be a British army cultural advisor. I was supposed to produce the five things you shouldn't do in front of Afghans: five bullet points. And that's indeed what most soldiers needed. But anyone in a command position or anyone who actually liaised with Afghans needed more. My boss said, "Explain Afghans to me." He was very stretched with a huge command, and he wanted a simple answer. The trouble is, there isn't one. He didn't just want me to translate language, but to translate culture, and it can't be done. He had to somehow get his head around how Afghan society worked, how decisions were made, where the power lay. It was not just the etiquette: that was the easy bit.*'

I think the word etiquette is interesting here. Chambers Dictionary defines it as 'forms of civilised manners or decorum . . . The conventional laws of courtesy observed between members of the same profession, sport, etc.' Laws that can be translated, simplified, codified, understood and applied. As I have thought more about CQ, I think a lot of leaders confuse it with etiquette. Learn the laws, job done. When, in fact, etiquette is just a starting point. Crucial, but basic. Not trivial, but by no means the end of the journey.

I went back to both Chris and Mike on this, and they agreed. Chris: '*A lot of people think etiquette is key to CQ. In some ways, it's true, but it's also trivial.*' Mike: '*Yes, many people in the military confuse CQ with etiquette. Especially older people. They tend to think that's all there is to it.*'

It isn't all there is to CQ. It isn't even all there is to Flex.

Flexing beliefs

As you go beyond behaviours and deeper into Flex, it gets even harder. Flexing how you behave is one thing, but Flexing what you believe gets very tough.

A while ago, I was invited to Jeddah, to work with a great women's university there. Women-only, I thought: I can cope with that. I wouldn't go to one to study, but it doesn't touch my Core. To get there, I would have to cover up completely, most of the time. This grates very seriously with everything I believe about the role of women in the world. My daughters were astonished that I would even contemplate it. I knew it was something I would find very hard to do. But, if I have to Flex on anything, I find clothes pretty easy, because I don't care about them. So that was easier for me than it might be for someone else. But I would also have to avoid driving, and behave discreetly. Right: we are really approaching my Core now, I thought. But I went, covered, completely, all in black, from head to toe.

And I learned a lot from doing it. I learned how much easier it is to be covered in a society where everyone looks at you. I discovered how women can make even a black full-length gown elegant if they want to. I realised how lovely it was to get off the streets into women-only areas, throwing the blackness off and making friends faster than normal, once we were all inside together. And it blew a huge bias out of my head. I had always thought – half consciously and half unconsciously – that all women who covered themselves must be weak. Subjugating themselves; too feeble to say no; too scared to resist.

I don't know about all women but, behind my black covering, I certainly met enough tough, able, interesting, pragmatic women for me never to make this generalisation again. Back at home, the experience helped me to have a timely conversation with an Arab man who was in London from the Middle East and was expressing his frustration about the forceful women he was having to deal with in the UK. He perceived the way they dressed as a lack of modesty and could not see around it to recognise their ability. I hope my experience of Flexing a belief I held very deeply helped him to do the same, because that's the point of Flex: you have to Flex there. First you move a belief from Core to Flex, and then you have to remember to Flex it, and keep Flexing it, even when you are bad-tempered, disheartened, offended or sometimes just tired.

So here's another example of mine. There is enough of me that is British to believe that you have to say 'please' pretty well all the time, and everywhere. If you don't, it's not polite. It took me a long time to figure out that people can be polite and not say 'please' all the time: they just have different ways of expressing their politeness. So saying 'please' went from my Core to my Flex. But . . . Recently, I was sitting in transit at JFK in New York. I was very tired, and everyone working there was being officious. I'd been barked at by a whole series of line organisers telling me where to stand or sit, not one of whom had said 'please' since I'd walked off the plane. As my bad temper brewed, I stopped myself. Hang on, this is Flex, I thought. Look for other signals that they are polite. And I found some. A kind smile as the order was shouted, an even kinder one when someone spotted how tired I was.

So, if this book has no impact on anyone else, it has at least taught me something. You have to Flex, and keep doing it. You also have to do it for real, in good faith, without flinching, or glazing over, or tutting, or sticking on a fixed grin. All of which simply transmit that you're not Flexing this belief at all.

As you establish something deeper than a set of codified behaviours, the real value of Flex emerges. When you get something wrong – as you inevitably will, with someone, somewhere – they will forgive you, and, instead of dismissing you, explain it to you.

But not too much Flex

Before we get carried away with Flex, remember this. If you're all Flex and no Core, no one will trust you (you may even end up not trusting yourself). To paraphrase Robert Frost, you can be 'too broadminded to take your own side in a quarrel'.

All Flex and no Core is as bad as all Core and no Flex. It can happen for many reasons, and sometimes with very good intentions:

1. You might want to show respect above everything else. So you adapt to everything and everyone. In your attempt not to upset anyone by showing the slightest bit of Core, you end up simply appearing ingratiating. Even if you're sincere, you can come across as insincere, and you can end up taking Flexing to a ridiculous degree. Many years ago, I went to an event in Belfast for young leaders. On the table were bowls of brightly coloured sweets. Someone had carefully removed all the sweets with orange wrappers, because orange is associated with the Unionist community, and all the green sweets, because green is associated with the Republican community. The organisers only got halfway through explaining why they'd done it before they twigged how ridiculous it was and started putting them all back in again.

2. Related to this is a less well-intentioned reason: the desire to prove how 'in' you are. Graham Boyce relates a story from his time in the Foreign Office. He once landed in a Middle Eastern country, to be greeted by the UK ambassador wearing full-flowing robes. Graham's first thought? It was probably time for the ambassador to move on to his next posting.

It's an extreme example. But lots of leaders fall into the trap of 'going native'. They lose sight of what their role is and who they are. It's a balancing act, but you have to be careful not to Flex so far that you tip over.

3. Avoiding too much Flex is particularly hard if you are an immigrant. Balancing the desire to integrate with the desire to hold on to your roots, for yourself and for your family, is very tough indeed. Shirlene Oh pinned it down for me: *'Without a Core, as a migrant, you try to adapt too much and you get lost, or you end up retreating to what was familiar and remain entrenched. You undermine your values, have no sense of what you believe in and you start to confuse yourself and others. You do unpredictable things and, in your eagerness to make friends and fit in, you can easily end up doing things for the wrong reasons.'*

I think I have never been more British than when I was a migrant in New York in my childhood. I felt so unwelcome that I retreated back into my Britishness, comforted by the knowledge that I would be going home.

Jon Williams is now Managing Editor for international news at ABC, based in New York, having been Foreign Editor at BBC News. He has worked among more migrant communities than most and describes it well: *'Remember, many migrants don't feel they come from anywhere. They just seek to belong to a place which is better than the one they have left.'*

In this situation, Flexing is the only option. The danger is that you Flex too far.

4. For some, the motivation is simply to avoid the polarisation that surrounds them in society. Like the students I spoke to in South Africa, people don't want any part of factions, or closed clubs, or sectarian divides of any kind. The danger is that, in their anger at what they see and their desire for something fresher and more open, they walk away from their Core, become all Flex, and float and drift away, and the real tragedy is that, as a result, no one trusts them.

5. And then there are leaders who are all Flex, almost in desperation. They have this funny feeling that, if they look too deep inside themselves, they will find they have very little Core left. So they simply stay in Flex forever and hope that it's enough to hide what's missing.

So Flex, both behaviours and beliefs, and keep Flexing, but don't Flex everything. You don't have to be in other people's shoes all the time to earn their trust. Sometimes you have to wear your own.

The ever-sliding scale

Once you've worked out what's Core and Flex for you, you need to keep reviewing them, testing, weeding, and transplanting, to make sure that the right things are in the right places, and that your Flex is actually Flexing. The sliding scale between them moves (or it should), and sometimes it can reveal things that are difficult for you.

Alan Lau in Hong Kong agrees: *'I think you do sometimes see things in too simple terms. You believe something is Core and don't recognise that it isn't, that you could have done something another way without compromising anything, and it's difficult when you discover it too late.'*

Reuel Khoza feels it too: *'My father was a preacher. I thought that I would always be a faithful partner, but I have found myself not to be, or not as faithful as I should have been. I have found myself trapped in doing the wrong thing, and I moved it to Flex and let it happen. But really it's deep enough in my Core that, though it has slid, I feel deeply troubled and guilty about it.'*

Mike Brearley's view: *'The trick is to balance being open to others and being true to yourself. It's not easy.'*

It's also different for everyone. So here's one that's in the balance for me right now.

For as long as I can remember, I have always signed off all my letters, emails and texts 'Love Julia'. I do this whether I know the recipient or not. I do it with anyone and everyone: family, CEOs, government ministers, emirs, bishops, neighbours, shopkeepers. Is this Core or is this Flex? Like instinctively wanting to touch people I'm talking to, is this essentially me? Is sending love and seeing all people as equal a behaviour which is so essential to my identity that to drop it would cut away at my Core and harm both me and my relationships? Or is this a behaviour that I should just grow out of, because it actually belongs firmly in Flex? Does my unwillingness to move it out of Core at best put up barriers with some people and at worst deeply offend them? I don't yet know the answer to this question. Like a lot of my own quest to develop CQ, I am still working on it, but I am aware of it. Myrna Atalla is CEO of Alfanar, which does venture philanthropy in the Arab world (I am a board member). I was talking to her recently, and mentioned my sign-off. She smiled at me kindly and, very quietly, said, 'Oh, so you do know.' She has no doubt had to deal with the unintended consequences more than once.

A leader who is looking to gain CQ is constantly working away on this sliding scale, testing and trying out, falling over and bouncing back, calibrating where it should be set, and when it should move, because that's how you get it.

It's not just about you

When we started looking at Core and Flex, I said the challenge was to look at yourself first, to establish what is Core and Flex for you, but this is only the first step. The point of doing all that is to enable you to go out and put your CQ to the test – with other people from different cultures – and then to continue doing it, adjusting appropriately as you proceed.

And, of course, the first thing that happens when you do this is that you meet other people with Cores and Flexes of their own. That's when it all gets more complex, and more real.

I think it is helpful to keep loosely in mind the three most obvious places you are likely to find yourself in.

- **You are both in Core**. Here, the room for manoeuvre could be quite tight, and the stakes quite high.

- **One of you is in Core and the other in Flex**. Here, you might get surprises. One person is feeling entirely comfortable, but the other person is not, so the first person could well go too far without noticing – until it's too late.

- **You are both in Flex**. Here, everything is pretty relaxed, but the interaction could be quite superficial. You aren't building trust, because that requires Core too.

All three are worth exploring a bit more.

Your Core, my Core

Sometimes you will be working together on an issue that touches your Core, and it touches the other person's Core too. You are in an area which is pretty solid for you both, and on which you have both decided that Flexing is pretty unlikely.

There are lots of examples of this, in pretty much every field. I asked an old friend, John Inge, the Bishop of Worcester, about faith, and about what happens when one faith meets a different one, and both are deep in Core. I asked John if a clash was inevitable: surely the evidence in the

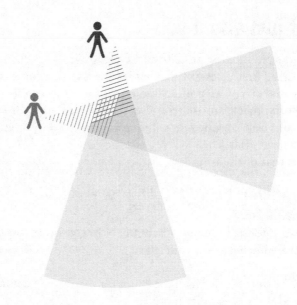

modern world is that the prospect of harmony is very slim? John tells me how wrong I am: *'Faith actually does the complete opposite to conflict: it brings people together, because all great faiths share in common the essence of humility and compassion. This connects people across many divides, all the time. For sure, some people seek to commandeer faith in order to divide people, but that is not really what faith is about. If the roots of your faith are deep and strong enough, you will certainly be strong enough to tear down the walls that divide you from others.'*

Graham Boyce's experience as an ambassador matches John's: *'I think it's important to accept that it is very unlikely that people from different cultures will have identical Cores. This must be the starting point. From there, you have to believe that you can find some common ground if you are determined to work at it, and that you will find a way to establish compatibility. Two countries won't agree on all things, but they will generally find enough. As an ambassador, you are watching to ensure that they don't actually clash.'*

Vidya Shah in Mumbai gave me an example from the private sector: *'We did a Joint Venture which combined the Japanese and Indian cultures. They are polar opposites. In India we love chaos, we thrive on it. It helps us to think. We believe that we are always overcoming adversity, and we are good at it. The*

Japanese managers set up project review meetings, with deliverables: this sent the Indian managers all over the place. Both have learned to adapt and appreciate the other. Now, we hold two regular meetings: a project review meeting which goes by the book, and an "ideation" meeting, where anything goes.'

I think this is useful wherever two Cores are in play, and it's not just across sectors, beliefs and geographies. I think an important (and easily overlooked) clash of Cores occurs between generations: where older people believe that their Core is more legitimate and therefore outweighs that of the young.

My Core, your Flex (and vice-versa)

This is territory most of us operate in every day, when all is going swimmingly, and then suddenly something you feel very relaxed and comfortable about suddenly hits someone else's Core.

Even within one culture, it can jolt. Across different cultures, it can shock: and can inadvertently destroy the trust you felt was being developed by the good atmosphere in the room. It can completely throw you, too. When you sign yourself off as 'Love Julia' and someone suddenly tells you (or, even worse, doesn't and you find out later) they are deeply offended, when you take your shoes off at the end of a long day and finally put your feet up and wiggle your toes – in front of an Arab who is sitting there, staring at you in horror.

Sometimes it can happen between cultures that don't seem far apart and perhaps even share the same language. As a family, we are all pretty freewheeling when it comes to swearing (you won't spend long with us without hearing the F word), but my husband objects to blasphemy. When my nieces visit from Canada, two interesting jolts happen. They are shocked by language they would never use at home, and they are even more shocked when their default 'Oh my God!' gets such a strong reaction. Their first response is to read it as inconsistency, but actually, it's Core and Flex clashing.

Occasionally the clash comes because people misunderstand why something is in the other person's Core. They assume that they know and then misread the situation. A simple example: drinking alcohol. I don't drink alcohol, never have. Some people are teetotal from conviction. For others, it's health. For others, it is part of their faith. For me, it is none of these: it is that, in my childhood, I saw too much of the damage alcohol does, and I simply could not bring myself to be anything but teetotal. It's not a decision; it's just the way it is for me. I am entirely relaxed about other people drinking, but mostly people assume any one of the other reasons and act with great care, when they simply don't need to.

Your Flex, my Flex

Personally, I find this the most difficult space to be in. Everyone is Flexing along nicely, so why spoil the cosy atmosphere by introducing a bit of Core? Or do they have any Core at all? It is indeed lovely when everyone works together and gets on, as long as progress is being made, trust is being built, and differences are not being ignored or politely papered over.

I remember some of my father's business colleagues, about 40 years ago. When they were in London, I would often be part of showing them around. I used to be given tasks like taking two members of the Chinese Walnut Trade Delegation to the House of Commons for the evening (I remember their bewilderment). One of my father's UK colleagues would usually come with us. To a man, they were of another generation. They were unbelievably courteous to people. Not supercilious and overbearing, nothing horrible; simply unbelievably courteous. They had learnt the customs of their guests, and they performed them with deep respect. They were utterly charming. And that's it. It was not negative; it was just grimly neutral and produced no lasting relationships and no friendships. Maybe the unfailing courtesy delivered solid deals, but, if the deals ever unravelled, I doubt there was anything there to build on that might have put them back together again.

My worry is that, if you stay in Flex, you are in danger of never touching the Core, so you never build trust in each other. My old boss used to tell me that all leaders are like teabags: *'You only know if they are any good when you put them in hot water'*. I think the same could be said for relationships. Until the Core is revealed, and shared on both sides, the trust will only ever be limited. Courteous, but skin-deep.

In the end, for me, figuring out how to operate in these intersections of Core and Flex comes down to four things:

- believing that all people have good qualities in both their Core and Flex, until you see real evidence to the contrary;

- being open to the fact that people are different: letting them have their own Core and not imposing yours on them;

- avoiding the trap of labelling people and only respecting the ones with the same Core as you;

- mastering the urge to avoid discomfort, and boxing it off into something you can cope with more easily.

But, as ever, a note of caution on all this, just in case it's all getting a bit too tidy, because we know that CQ very much isn't.

With all his experience of working around the globe, Etienne de Villers tells me that sometimes leaders use apparent Core as a smokescreen. He describes doing business in parts of Asia Pacific, where Core can be presented as overwhelming, complex, mystical, deep and opaque, and so fundamentally different that even the greatest Flexer could never hope to understand it.

Etienne says that you sometimes need to be careful not to fall into the trap of believing this. The opaqueness can sometimes be a deliberate act to prevent you from understanding. It is used to distract you, unnerve you and, ultimately, to disarm you, and he is pretty dismissive about this tactic. He believes that Core is *'important as glue, and even as a shield. But it should not be used as a sword.'*

His advice is to remember that very few people are really that fundamentally different. His approach when doing a deal is: *'Wait them out. Wait for all the veneer – the false Core – to work its way through. Then do a good deal, or don't do a deal at all.'*

Maria Figueroa Kupcu in New York has a rather more light-hearted example of this kind of cultural opacity from her family: *'I am the wife (aged 42) of an eldest son (aged 44). So, while his younger brother (aged 43) is older than me, the expectation is that he should more often call me (rather than expect me to call him). In this case, marriage trumps age. These kinds of rituals create an expected pattern, and can make things easier inside the group, but they generally baffle outsiders.'*

I think Core and Flex are very useful notions. It's good to work out what's in your own, and it's essential to try to understand what they mean for other people in other places and from different backgrounds.

The endless interplay between them is at the centre of every meeting, every negotiation and every attempt to build a bridge to someone else. I would argue that it will also be at the centre of every successful organisation. Individual CQ can aggregate in organisations that are smart enough to realise its value.

Chris Mathias agrees: *'I think organisations have Core and Flex too, and, in many ways, it's the element that distinguishes them. Is Goldman the most powerful financial house in the world because of the size of their balance sheet, or their financial firepower, or their geographic spread? None of the above, really. I think it's because they have a clear, common, deeply embedded Core. That is their strength, and their Core is so strong that they then Flex with ease and confidence in different geographies around the world. I have seen them at work in India, the US and Europe. I've seen the same Core and how they Flex differently in each one. In the UK, for example, they are entirely buttoned-down, but in India they have masses of "Jugaad" – a creative or innovative idea that provides a quick, alternative way of solving a problem, which you need there. Having said that I observe geographical CQ at Goldman, I don't see a great deal of CQ in how they work with women!'*

As I've said more than once already, CQ isn't easy, but it always starts with the individual, which is where we go next.

Exercise: Assess your own Core and Flex

Later in the book, we will look at Core and Flex in more depth. For now, before you read on, it would be interesting to put this book down, get a piece of paper and list your own Core and Flex. If you need something to get you going, the following might help:

1. **List things that you really don't mind:**

   what I look like
   what car I own
   having to wait for people
   the sight of blood
   what I wear

When you've got your list, go back and, after each entry, briefly write down – just for yourself – why.

2. **Write a list of sentences starting with 'I would never . . .'**

Think about values, behaviours, skills, beliefs and identity: the lot. List them fast. Don't stop to put them in any order. Here are some examples, but write your own:

I would never . . .

   smile at a stranger
   question someone who is older than me
   grow long hair
   question an order
   swear
   marry outside my community
   be unwelcoming
   eat without washing my hands first
   use public transport

After each entry, write down – just for yourself – why.

3. Turn the tables round. Think about how others perceive you. Complete the sentence: 'People assume that I am . . .'

After each entry, write down – again, just for yourself – what this reveals to you about your Core or Flex.

4. Draw a dividing line between your Core and Flex where you think it currently lies. Then draw a second line indicating where you think it was five years ago.

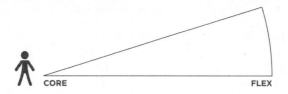

Part Four

The prerequisites

The CQ paradox

Before we get to the prerequisites for developing CQ, we need to deal with a paradox, and this is it: CQ comes from experience. Reading helps, but the majority of CQ comes through experience, and from other people: people who are very different from you, who engage with you and who choose to reveal their knowledge, their history, their stories, their aspirations, their rituals, their beliefs and their limits to you. Their Flex and, ultimately, their Core.

As Peter Kulloi in Budapest says, '*You have to trust people enough to ask them to explain a culture to you. Then they have to trust you enough to explain a culture to you. Both are important and generous judgement calls.*'

The problem is, they won't trust you unless they believe that you have some CQ. So, in order to get it, you have to have some in the first place. It's impossible: a circle that can't be squared. But, I'd argue, that's what leaders do.

And the good news is that once CQ starts to build, then it flows fast and furiously and you develop more and more at great speed. It snowballs. The more CQ you have, the more CQ you get. And what you learn allows you to operate across many different cultures.

To be a leader with CQ, you need three crucial prerequisites (and probably even a fourth). They have to be in your Core, and there is not much point in proceeding with CQ – or indeed with this book – without them.

The first is a deep interest in other people, and it needs to be deep enough that you avoid seeing yourself as the benchmark against which they should be judged.

The second is a determination to get to the bottom of what, in yourself, makes you feel either superior or inferior to other people at different times, or in different situations.

The third is the stamina to proceed on a very long and sometimes pretty painful journey with no end destination.

And I think that the fourth is a preparedness to stand up when you see the opposite of CQ in play, and that opposite is cultural intolerance.

A deep interest in other people

I actually believe this is a prerequisite for *all* successful leadership, but it is even more important for leaders who are looking to develop CQ. You need a fundamental interest in other people: all people, both people who are like you and people who are not like you.

This deep interest in other people probably comes if you have less sense of ego yourself. Peter Kulloi puts it well: '*In my experience, it's always ego that gets in the way of understanding people and learning to judge situations correctly. And it is the reason why people behave wrongly. They start to believe their own story. They believe in their own importance. They think they are smarter, richer and more powerful, and they get lazy about other people. So many fights are ego fights.*' Peter says you have to have the 'backbone' to keep ego in check. His example amazed me: '*However late I am, however bad the jam, however slow the traffic, however tight the bottleneck, and even if the police and the cameras that could catch me didn't exist, I would never use the bus lane. Who am I to put myself above others? Why am I more special than any of the other seven billion people on this earth? Why do I deserve special privileges? No. I would never go into a bus lane.*'

Alan Rosling worked for Tata in India for many years. He gave me another powerful example: '*I love Tata, and I loved working for Ratan Tata, a man who is stratospheric in his power and would never for a minute think of jumping a queue. He will always go to the back of it. He always had the spine to do the right thing.*'

Etienne de Villiers puts it his way: '*You have to respect that other people have a life, that their existence is as important as yours. That they have just as much right to be on this earth as you do.*'

Actor Riz Ahmed agrees: '*The breakthrough is when you discover that you are not the centre of the universe. We see ourselves as the lead character in a film about ourselves. At best, you are a bit part, and it's best to be a bit part, because they are usually full of character. The main characters tend to get caught in their role.*'

If you can keep your own ego under control, you are more likely to become fascinated by other people. You listen harder, you concentrate totally, you question gently and watch more carefully. You follow their movements and jump into step with them. You reflect their smiles and gobble up their stories. You dance their dances and eat their food. You hear their silences, hold their anger and understand their fears. You catch their ideas and pick their brains. And, very slowly, other people start telling you that you have an 'instinct with people'. It's not instinct, it's experience, born of deep interest.

This brings us to the essence of this prerequisite, which is to stop looking at other cultures, generations, sectors, geographies, faiths and races merely as variants of your own. Where yours is the main brand and theirs simply a line extension. As my father used to say: '*Most people travel to discover the world. Americans travel to explain America to the rest of the world.*' I wouldn't limit this attitude to Americans. You find people like this everywhere.

To have any chance of getting other people to trust you, so that they can really teach you CQ, they need to be equals, not just variants of you, and what you know, and how you do things. You are not the benchmark. You are not even a benchmark.

Shirlene Oh gives a good East–West example: '*A Chinese person adapts to the situation. There is no need for a detailed plan at this point, they cry, but we must know the destination. If you change the "how" as you go along, that's fine. A Westerner reads this as inconsistency. What the Chinese person sees as going with the flow – with a clear end goal in mind, weaving, finding the points of least resistance, progressing – the Westerner sees as a looming mess, led by a fickle leader. The Chinese person's analogies will be about flowing water: about being resourceful and dealing with problems as they arise, but keeping the water flowing. To suggest that you can anticipate the problems up ahead is almost silly to them. Of course, the answer is a bit of both approaches; but, to find it, both sides have to hear, accept and adapt, not paper over, or dismiss. People don't like adapting, because they feel that their way has led to success. We need to be much more pluralistic in our approach.'*

Eric Thomas agrees that you shouldn't see your position as the default position for everyone else, but he also points out that different people have a lot in common: *'My brother has lived in Japan for 33 years so I have visited there often. It's a very different world, but a world in which parents love their kids and they love their own mums and dads. They work hard, come back home exhausted and watch too much TV. There is one thing people the world over love to talk about and that is their families. We might eat differently, or talk differently, but you do get to the cretinously simple conclusion that we are all pretty much the same. The realisation makes people less foreign.'*

Twenty-four-year-old Iranian Shirin Gerami flew from London back to Iran to get permission from the Iranian government to be the first official Iranian female athlete to run the World Triathlon Championships. She spent a week persuading people, always 'remaining positive' (as one man told her to all the way through, however impossible it might have felt to get all the permissions in time). And she worked with a tireless tailor in Tehran who was determined to help her to get her kit designed and made in time for the competition back in London. I asked her how she did it: *'I drew on my experience of cycling a rickshaw in London, all through the previous winter. The customers came from every corner of the earth and society. There were rich guys and snobbish guys, hipsters, homeless people and thieves, and everyone in between. It taught me that there is absolutely no one you can't connect with and reach out to.'*

This combination of a lack of ego, an interest in people and a willingness to be one of many equals rather than the benchmark will tempt others to generosity, and that's what helps to square the circle of how to acquire CQ.

A determination about yourself

I also think that leaders have to dig deep and figure out what makes them feel superior or inferior to other people in certain situations. Whether conscious or subconscious, these feelings get in the way.

Superiority translates rapidly into exchanges with other people that leave them feeling offended or patronised.

Mike Brearley again: '*Lots of people distinguish themselves from others through a hierarchy: I am above or below you. People with CQ don't. They don't put people above or below; and they won't let people do it to them either. Authority can be a barrier to CQ too: because it means that people won't reveal things to you. So if you want CQ, you really have to drop authority – even if you have it.*'

Perversely, feelings of inferiority can create exactly the same outcome. Arun Maira gave me a very good example from India: '*I once found myself in charge of a merger between two struggling companies. It was a condition of the merger that I became Chairman. Both sides said they wanted me because it would bring two very different cultures together, and I was the most tolerant person they knew. What they had not seen was how intolerant I can be when I'm faced with intolerance. They were extraordinarily intolerant of anyone with a different world view from theirs. They were deeply disrespectful of anything they felt did not fit their way of thinking. I think the attitude was born of the sense of inferiority they felt when the two original companies were in trouble. But, as soon as we began to make progress, their superiority became almost as frightening. They looked down on anyone they associated with the past.*'

Mark Moran is the former Chief Executive of Mater Hospital in Dublin. He gave me another compelling take on inferiority. I asked him how he spotted when the British were about to patronise him. He simply turns it round: '*If you look for it, you'll find it, and then it becomes your problem. So don't go looking for it because you are then halfway convinced before you start.*' And if it does happen and you are patronised? '*Just laugh,*' he said. '*Because then it's their problem, not yours. Feel sorry for their ignorance.*'

But, for many people, this can be a very long journey. I spoke with Firoz Patel as he completed a Common Purpose programme which had taken him to Mumbai. Now in his 40s, and the founder and Chief Executive of Childreach International, Firoz was born in a small village in India. His grandfather was a policeman for the Raj. He left India when he was 13 and came to the UK. As it has for so many in the Indian Diaspora, Bollywood kept him connected to India and he has returned to Mumbai every year since he left. '*But this trip was different,*' he said. '*I came in a group drawn from 28 countries; among the members of the group were some important African leaders. Those of us from India and Africa spent many hours together, in the evenings and well into the nights. We talked about what we had done and seen that day, but also about how we had responded ourselves, and how we had observed each other respond. On the programme, we saw what Mumbai is now, where it is going, the momentum it has built up and its unwillingness to wait for anyone or anything. We met Indian leaders who are confident, strident, opinionated and full of conviction. And we saw the Westerners in our group trying to catch up; seeing hope everywhere and trying to be part of the dynamism and urgency of it. We began to realise that – because of the similar experiences we had all been through in India and Africa – if you are brought up in a colony, you often end up feeling inferior. You feel that somehow Westerners are better than you. You almost buy the concept that the Western colonisers were there to civilise you, because you needed civilising. After all, it took only a few hundred thousand of them to control millions of us for decades. In Mumbai last week, we made a pact. We all decided to drop this feeling inferior stuff.'*

Firoz saw the same thing happening in Mumbai: *'For the first time ever, the Indians we met didn't look past us – as they always have in the past – to the Westerners we were with. They wanted to talk to us. I realised that my sense of inferiority has coloured my view of the world for years. I think I have always had quite a lot of CQ, but I think I will now have far more because I feel equal to others. We are level now. I won't let myself get in the way.'* And then he laughed: *'You know, the traffic in Mumbai just about slows down for people who are taking their lives into their hands to cross bursting, honking roads. But it won't stop. Not for anyone. Not even for Westerners.'*

Matt Hyde was Chief Executive of the National Union of Students and is now Chief Executive of the Scout Association in the UK. He has long experience of the interaction between the generations and he gave me a useful cautionary note about people playing down to stereotype: *'Basically, be level with people. Avoid being above or below, and don't skew it yourself. If young people play the "young person act" they bring it upon themselves. Playing the naive, admiring "I just don't know" act encourages patronising behaviour. If you play the child, established leaders will just go into parenting mode.'*

For all this, I know full well that both Mark and Firoz are sure to have their own moments of superiority too, perhaps rooted somewhere in bits of their past that haven't surfaced yet, because we all do, and these can easily lead to bias. Dr Robert Care is Australian, and Chair of Arup

UKMEA. He agrees: *'Yes, you do discover your own biases as you go through life. The important thing is that, when you notice them, you do something about it. Sometimes I like to hope it's not even bias; it's just inexperience, or a blind spot.'*

A former Australian Army officer, Matt Jones is now Executive Director of Social Alchemy in Sydney. He openly admits to bias too: *'I now see diversity in a new light. I have always thought of people as where they come from: Korean, Turkish, Zambian. Now it's far more complex, with multiple layers. I admit to becoming aware of my own personal bias, which previously I wasn't aware of, or at least did not acknowledge. But, standing in a room full of Africans for the first time – not just a handful of Africans (which I had plenty of experience of) but a whole room of Africans – was a profound experience. I cringe slightly as I say this: I know you will think that I have led my life hiding under a rock, but I haven't, far from it. This was new. We all have bias; we just probably don't know what form it takes.'*

As Area Commander for the British Transport Police in Scotland, Ellie Bird has spent years policing around the most toxic areas of cities: their main railway stations. She is succinct on the need to watch out for sectarianism: *'It's built on people feeling superior, and inferior. Both make people aggressive.'*

I think that to develop CQ, you have to be prepared to make these discoveries about yourself, and slowly even out the playing field until it becomes level.

It is certainly better to level with yourself and make sure you're level with people you meet.

Recently, I gave a speech to 50 disabled students doing a Common Purpose course. They were bright, quick, witty – and ruthless in their reactions to me and to what I said. The session went well, and I wanted to make sure that I would get it right again next time, so I asked the course leader, Genevieve Barr, for feedback. I knew that she would be completely honest, because she had taken me to pieces plenty of times when things hadn't gone so well.

She told me: *'You are candid and unapologetically so, and that resonates with disabled people more than anything. With every question, you only have a "can do" attitude: there is always a way round something. And, for you, there's nothing wrong with failure or being wrong sometimes. I remember talking to you about careers when I was 20, and I had no idea what I wanted to do. And you said, very bluntly, that I needed to think about what I couldn't do because of my deafness, and how I was going to work around it. Ironically, by being so blunt, far from thinking what I couldn't do because I was deaf, I've ended up doing what I can do because I'm deaf. And I've become a better person because of it.'*

I think, back then, I judged Gen right, and I suspect it was because I was simply not conscious of speaking to a disabled person, just to a very smart and determined young woman. For me, Reuel Khoza crystallises it all best: *'I was born in a rustic part of South Africa. I am only interested in the human element of people. For me, to be human is sufficient, and to have material things is superfluous. I don't care what you have or don't have. I neither admire you for your wealth, nor dismiss you for your poverty. The best is to have courageous conversations with people who think like this too. But if you don't, that won't change me.'*

This is all easily said, hard to achieve and may be impossible to complete, but it is crucial to aspire to.

The stamina for an endless journey

The journey to CQ is a long, slow and messy one. Yet, for most of us in most situations, speed is of the essence. Everything worth doing must have a Key Performance Indicator. So it is very difficult to embark on a journey that doesn't, because there is no formula, no end point, no 'got it' moment. The CQ comes through the journey and the attitude of a leader who accepts this, who understands that there is always more to learn, to question and to be curious about; more to unpick, unlock and put back together again. The moment leaders think that they have 'got it' with CQ is the moment they throw away what they have learned.

CQ is full of questions with no answer, and it is because they have no answer that we need CQ.

IQ is so much easier. It's not quite 'you have it or you don't' – but it's not far off, and, compared with CQ, it's very simple. There is even a test.

A fixed point that gives you a score: a percentile ranking, compared with everyone else, that you carry around with you to prove it. CQ is very different. With CQ, there is no test. (I don't count Air Miles, even if some leaders think that's their Key Performance Indicator). Maybe one test could be whether you spot the opportunities to learn from people, rather than walk past them or dismiss them. I am convinced that I would fail Peter Kulloi's 'bus lane' test for sure.

Mike Brearley told me about long hard journeys that call for slowing down and taking time, and he gave me another wonderful saying. If you come across leaders who expect to be told to 'do something', sometimes you have to say: *'Don't just do something. Stand there.'*

It's like that with cultures. They're complicated and ever-changing. Like people, they mix and merge, so the learning is messy and inconsistent. You can't be impatient for answers if you want the real ones.

Adam Habib in Johannesburg describes it eloquently: *'Get your head around it: cultures are not homogeneous but heterogeneous. There is no such thing as "an African solution" to an African problem. There is always a plurality of interpretations of different cultures. The differences are not a product of race, or class, or any one factor. They're the result of different people facing different problems, in the context of different historical challenges that weave into different cultural architectures, and find themselves set against different value systems and historical traditions, with different institutional architectures and political structures. It all stretches back over thousands of years and it all results in how a person thinks. It also guarantees that different people end up with different solutions to the same problems.'*

Riz Ahmed in New York agrees: *'You have to be very brave. You have to face up to all the accusations: about what you have said or done that is blinkered, or because you have camouflaged something and tried to ignore it. You have to mine your own prejudices and not shut them down. You have to cope with the confusion – and Flex with it. I think CQ is hugely confusing, but what comes from it is inspiration. There is no cultural GPS system: just cope with the mess.'* It drives him mad when people want simplicity: *'They keep banging on about consistency. How can you be consistent if you are many different things? It's an illusion anyway. The only thing worth being consistent about is your Core.'* He laughs: *'Aldous Huxley had it right: "Consistency is a virtue for trains".'*

This seems a good place to discuss something that has come up again and again in my discussions about CQ with leaders all over the world: the widespread feeling that Americans struggle with it. Which, for a country of immigrants, seems completely illogical to many observers. Though Ron Arculli rightly points out in the introduction to this book that there are exceptions, I wanted to get my head around it. So I spent some time speaking to leaders in America. But, finally, it was Vidya Shah in Mumbai who helped me the most: '*The US relationship with the past is something we so badly need in India. I think the US succeeds because it has shed its legacy, cut it all off at the roots. In India, we are stuck in our past and we have a total inability to shed our legacy. We can't let go of institutions, concepts, notions which no longer serve us. So our devotion to the past is our weakness. Then again, the US ability to move on also gives it a weakness. They do not understand cultures which are rooted in the past. They see history as "fuss" to be swept aside and moved on from. As a result, they can sometimes inadvertently show a lack of respect.*'

I have become fascinated by the idea that it is actually everything which is most admirable about the US and its citizens that can cause them to be weak at CQ. Here is my logic:

1. In the US, what you see is what you get, so it's hard for Americans to understand that in some cultures, you have to start a conversation with a (sometimes quite lengthy) dance. You have to go deeper, and spend longer, before you get to what people are really saying.

2. Americans look at history in a different way. As one leader there explained to me: '*In the US, we are less influenced by history. It's something you dump rapidly over your shoulder once you have read about it, so that you can keep on pioneering.*' History – and all the old divisions that comprise it – is Old World thinking, and many Americans feel they have moved on from it, so they don't naturally look to history for understanding or explanations, as many cultures do. Indeed, a lot of Americans distrust cultures that see history in this way.

3. Assimilation is the abiding cultural narrative in the US. The deal is that you must subordinate your own customs and laws. You 'do culture' at home, but at work – and even in school – you harmonise with American-ness and the American Way. This, combined with

the desire to succeed (and the possibility that, because of relative social mobility, you *can* succeed) means that you get this overwhelming drive to assimilate in the US. This leaves less space for understanding other cultures, or even feeling the need to.

4. Americans are individualistic by nature. Many people have said to me that if Americans want to get something done, they are likely to go to an individual to make it happen, rather than gather a group. So creating the networks you need to develop CQ (especially the turbulent networks) is not instinctive.

5. Americans are philanthropists. They get engaged, and they give their time and money to solve problems. Their spirit of generosity is glorious, but it can be perceived as overwhelming (or patronising, or even condescending) in other cultures.

6. Americans love moving to action and solving problems. Anything that delays this is not to be trusted. But some cultures are more reflective at the outset, and certainly quieter. They can be drowned out by a strident, confident voice with a plan of action that can't wait to get things going.

I have a feeling that these characteristics make acquiring CQ difficult. It's not that Americans don't have the capability – some, of course, excel at it – but they are programmed differently. It is a bigger ask for them.

Allyson Stewart-Allen is a Californian who has been based in Europe for over 20 years. She is also the co-author of *Working with Americans*,[1] a book about US business culture. I ran this logic past her. She smiled, and added: '*In the USA, we are all US citizens, so I don't need to know context, because the rules apply irrespective of context, and it's the same for all of us. The deal has always been that you give up the ways of the land you have left for this land that you have adopted. And the US does things inclusively: the American Way. That's what inclusion means in the US: common to all. I arrived at Logan airport, having flown first class, and I asked for the passport fast-track. "We don't do that," they told me. "You are like everyone else, get in line." The American Way is the Core – and it doesn't need to Flex.*'

One thing is certain: CQ is a journey on which you are guaranteed to make a fool of yourself and, at worst, make horrible mistakes that deeply offend people (like when you kiss an imam). A journey with traps galore. I asked my daughter to describe someone she had just met. She told me, '*He is nice and tall, and wears a bow tie and has a bit of a stoop.*' And then added nervously, '*and he is black. But is it racist to say that?*' In the UK, the fear of saying anything wrong almost prevents communication.

It's also a journey on which you will hear things you don't want to hear. You will have to survive knocks and humiliations. You will have to forgive others their mistakes. Worst of all, you will have to forgive yourself your own mistakes.

Gavin Dyer is Sales and Marketing Director for Weir Minerals in South Africa. He knows this full well: '*Over the last 13 years, I have been doing a lot of late-in-life education, and it has accelerated because of Common Purpose. I have an awakening respect for culture, and different cultures. People do things differently in different countries and different workplaces. It seems obvious, but it wasn't obvious to me, and it has been hard discovering just how stupid I have been.*'

You will also have to learn to reveal your mistakes, in the hope that others will reveal theirs to you. It all takes time.

Konstantin Mettenheimer is Chairman for all Edmond de Rothschild's businesses in Germany. He agrees: '*The trust that is crucial to CQ takes time. It can very occasionally be instantaneous: if you see someone saving someone else from drowning, for example. But mostly it is built over time, through constancy.*' I'm not sure Riz would agree. '*There is a long way between the outer shell of the brain and the inner core of the heart.*'

I'll give the last word on this to Bella Matambanadzo, Chief Executive of the Zimbabwe Trust, a non-profit supporting the country's economic recovery. She said to me, '*I agree that CQ is a long journey, with no destination, but there are stopovers, where you have to sit back for a moment, and recognise just how far you have come.*'

Stand up to cultural intolerance

Now for the difficult one. You acquire CQ from other people, because they generously offer it to you. I think a key prerequisite is that you will, on occasion, have to stand up because you see the opposite of CQ.

Crude, offensive, harmful bigotry: cultural intolerance. Or possibly ignorant, blind laziness: cultural ignorance (though sometimes the two are hard to tell apart). You will have to say and do something, and not simply walk by.

Many years ago, a black colleague took me to task, and what she said has stuck with me ever since. I did not enjoy hearing it and I still wrestle with it 20 years on. She came into my office, sat down and said, *'Look Julia, I know you are one of the least prejudiced people I know, and I like that a lot. I have never seen you dismiss anyone. Indeed, I have seen you seek people out who are different from you and take the time to hear them, and understand them, and work with them. That's great. Well done. But all this means nothing to me if you don't stand up when you see prejudice in others and say something, ask questions which need asking, or take on people who need taking on. Only then should you take pride in the fact that you are relatively unprejudiced, and only then will I have any real time for you.'*

I asked Shirlene Oh if she felt the same: *'Yes, I think that's right. I think I would trust someone more if they were prepared to stand up, albeit in a non-confrontational and sensitive way. I would certainly trust them less if they remained silent while someone expressed offensive prejudice in front of me.'* She added, *'I don't think CQ can be passive. You learn, and you change your behaviour.'*

Alan Lau in Hong Kong is clear too: *'There is no option: you have to stand up if you come across cultural intolerance. You have to stand up, knowing that you cannot change the person but because you must talk to the others who are within hearing. If you don't, and you cover things over, then other people will cover things over as well. I believe that if you don't confront issues, you create a culture where real issues are not addressed.'*

Many people have said to me that there are times to say something and times not to; that you have to use your judgement in every situation; that it would be impolite to challenge a host, that with most people there is no point, because they will not change, and that you can make your point in other ways later. I think I disagree with them.

I have a feeling that many of these people (with some very notable exceptions, two of whom are mentioned below) are of my generation. No one from the generation younger than me has had any hesitation in agreeing that you must challenge. Anu Omideyi is a young black

British defence barrister. Her take on this is, as always, forthright: '*The older generation say nothing because, to them, it's an interesting discussion, not part of their life story. A conversation about the world we live in, not a do-or-die issue. The moment is minimal and fleeting; why would they say anything? And I am sad to say that others keep quiet because they think "me and mine have pushed through cultural intolerance, fought a good fight for ourselves and our families, and now we are doing just fine." So cultural intolerance is no longer their problem.*'

Some of these younger people go so far as to say that if you don't stand up and speak out, your CQ journey will grind to a halt. My generation does seem to want, above all else, to keep things calm and quiet, and on an even keel. One exception is Ron Arculli, in Hong Kong. He described it to me like this: '*Very few of my generation were brought up to be confrontational. We find different ways to say things, which sometimes means the moment is lost, or we water things down. The decision to make a stand is often a split-second one. In some cases, you are also so shocked by what has been said – sometimes by people you respect in all other things and they have surprised you – that you feel the need to check that you have heard it right before reacting. So that, by the time you are clear on what you will say, 30 seconds have been lost, and you think you will appear stupid or heavy-handed if you come back to it. But yes, I think you still must.*'

Another exception is Reuel Khoza in South Africa: '*I can't see something I believe to be wrong without saying something about it. This gets me in a lot of trouble as I pop my mouth. It's rooted in a deep sense of justice and injustice. If I see what I believe to be a travesty of justice, I speak out. In my world, the 30 seconds lost is not an issue. Sometimes I can wait for three months to say something, because I am waiting for the bigger moment. Don't be a cog. It may be brutal and bruising not to be, but I would rather die battered and bruised for a cause I stand for.*'

Konstantin Mettenheimer in Germany agrees: '*To grasp the 30 seconds and get it right, you have to be quite aggressive and on your toes. On the whole, leaders in high positions don't jump instantly and are more reflective. And, after all, most people do nothing, because it is easiest to do nothing. They say to themselves, "This is not my fight, why should I tell him off, risk his anger, lose his friendship?"*' But he is entirely clear: '*You simply have to come back. Maybe if it's a very small slip then you can let it go, but otherwise you have to say something.*'

I also think that a lot of the people who don't agree that standing up to cultural intolerance is a prerequisite for CQ have, on the whole, been in the majority for most of their lives. So their experience of being in a minority is very limited, and they have rarely been on the receiving end of it. Chris Mathias explains what it's like: '*Should you stand up to cultural intolerance? Only if it's in your Core. My daughters came home having received some snide racist comments on the tube. They had ignored them. I couldn't ignore them. It's not in my Core to say nothing, I never would: they set my fuse off. I don't lose it; I stay in control and I don't lose my temper, but I won't let it pass. I live in Surrey: there are loads of Hooray Henrys who say stupid things, make racist jokes, use offensive descriptors. I always push back, and they always back off and say they didn't mean it. And that's fine, I have made my point. I have to fight, because otherwise I would walk out. But all my daughters would say nothing. They tell me, "Dad, it's their problem, not mine." If it's not in their Core to fight it, then they won't, and to force it wouldn't work, because they would only be doing it for me. Maybe it will go into their Core when they have husbands or kids. Why is it in my Core? Because I don't mind confrontation, so my threshold for action is lower. Perhaps because I came to Britain in 1977, when it was horribly racist. At one stage, as a young accountant, the client even tried to get me off the job I was on because of my race. If he had succeeded and my partner had not backed me, I would have resigned. It's hard to imagine those days now. I was a proud young man and they probably radicalised me.*'

For my part, I am very aware of taking people on and making a total fool of myself. I still smart from many humiliating experiences of challenging prejudice that ended in abject failure. Getting myself into the wrong when it was, in fact, the other person who was. Letting outrage bubble out incoherently. Saying too much, or saying it in a whining voice. Letting anger cloud things. And it is all much worse if you are not making a point of theory, but instead one of personal experience, or if you are defending someone else, especially someone you love. I suspect I was better at taking on people who are prejudiced about disability before I had children who are disabled. Now, I come across as an angry shrill mother, outraged by ignorance and by how easy it is to crush someone.

But I have a feeling you just have to keep on doing it, and get better at it. You have to say something or do something, not to convert the bigot, but to flag up that you are not on their side. Crucially, you have to do it for the people around them, who need to know that you will stand by your Core and not simply write slides about 'values'. I suspect that the next generation sees it differently, not just because they are younger, but perhaps because they are frustrated by my generation.

I go back to Mike Brearley's expression: *'Don't just do something, stand there.'* Applied to prejudice, I don't think this means stand there in silence. I think it means don't rush to action. Don't change the subject, just to fill the moment. Don't jump to comfortable ground, where you are not embarrassed. Don't move on, or cover up, or sweep way, and remember that silence is not quiet. It's noisy, invasive, disruptive. Silence is very loud when a bigot speaks. And even louder when a good person stays silent.

You also have to get better at saying the right thing, in Ron Arculli's 30-second window to respond. I once did. I was at an event in a northern UK city, sitting in a row of speakers. I was about to be introduced as the first one. The mayor (who was doing the introductions) leaned over and whispered in my ear, *'Do you mind if I make a slightly sexist joke when I introduce you?'*. I turned to the man on my right who had overheard the whisper, and I said, *'You are next after me. Do you mind terribly if he makes a racist joke when he introduces you?'* Oooooh, what fun. Usually I think of the right thing to say in the dead of night, when the moment is long gone.

So I asked the advice of people I thought might get this moment right more often than I do. Even when you are taken aback, surprised, confused, worried, uncertain and needing to check what you've just heard, how do you get the response right? This is what they told me:

Arun Maira: *'It is always difficult to speak up. Whether this be to an individual or to a system. There are many moments when you let things go, but there are also ones when you are very sure, sure that you are doing it not just for yourself, but for the sake of all. When you do speak up, make your point and make sure you repeat it. Also, don't yell it.'*

Michael Hastings, KPMG's Global Head of Citizenship and Diversity: *'Don't use too many words. If you do, the other person will get it over on you. I have given up on clever responses, they come too late – usually in the middle of the night – and you can't wait for them. I say something brief and straight. I imply that it is cultural ignorance, rather than cultural intolerance. I do this, even if I know it's the latter, but it gives them a way out while making the point clearly. I offer to discuss it at a later date if they want to, because the situation is too heated. If you do too much in the heat of the moment, they will become even more charged. I try to keep clearly in my mind that the objective is to make them stop, not to convert them. They are more than likely beyond that, so my expectations remain low, but I won't just let it go.'*

Martin Kalungu-Banda: *'If you are taking on cultural intolerance, your primary objective is not to convert the guilty party. Your primary objectives are to make it clear that they have crossed a line beyond which you will not go, and to send the same message to the other people in the room. But if you can do this in a way that achieves it but also makes the guilty party interested in what has just happened in the room, then it is a greater win. If you just crush them, they will not be interested. It is very difficult to do, so most of us hide behind politeness and do not count the cost of doing nothing.'*

Konstantin Mettenheimer: *'People who say culturally intolerant things usually say them again. It's a pattern. So, if you missed the moment, wait; it will come again for sure. I heard someone say something anti-Semitic at a board meeting and I missed it the first and second times. But the third time I caught it, and I was ready. I wouldn't wait for a clever line: sometimes by giving a clever response, you can make a joke of it and, before you know it, you have achieved the opposite of your intention – you have inadvertently joined his camp. Make your point quickly, and don't over-explain. Be strong enough to catch him, but don't overdo it. My mother was a lioness: she would lie lazily in the sun and then suddenly jump. She would say something like "that was entirely inappropriate" or "you should know that . . ." or "did you not study history?"'*

Eric Thomas: *'My wife is very direct. Someone used the expression "ragheads" the other day, and she said, "I would be glad if you did not use that expression, please." It certainly works with the perpetrator, even if it's only temporarily. Without doubt, it emboldens other people to say things too.'* He also added one further piece of advice of his own: *'Whatever you say, say very little. Avoid getting drawn in.'*

But you have to say something. Because otherwise you feel dirty, and somehow corrupted by what's going on, and because it does make you feel good to get it right. Mostly, in the UK, you don't get the opportunity, because people cover their cultural intolerance with an elegant veneer: they know the language not to use and they don't use it. Eric agrees: *'The truth is, I don't get many opportunities to stand up to cultural intolerance. Not that it doesn't exist, but people have learned to disguise it. They know what not to say, even if it's what they think.'*

Bella Matambanadzo told me that she loves all this advice, but she warns me to be careful too: *'Sometimes you can be offensive without meaning to be. Accused of cultural intolerance yourself. I said to someone recently that I would not give her a role because I didn't want her to fail, because, given the role, only someone who looked like me would be successful in it at this moment. She was furious, because she said that I had been racist.'*

I said at the beginning of this section that I wasn't sure that standing up to cultural intolerance was the fourth prerequisite, but I think I have convinced myself, with one caveat.

Riz Ahmed said to me: *'You be careful, Julia, telling people to stand up to cultural intolerance. You are going to sound like a Victorian explorer, a worldly Western female explorer, intolerant in your fight against intolerance. You will have your own blinkers. There is no such thing as cultural neutrality. The only thing that will save you is if you don't treat your position as the default position. The best is not yours. Look at French liberalism, which becomes so evangelical that it becomes intolerance. You should challenge your own intolerance before you challenge others.'*

And he wasn't the only one to give me a warning. Kuben Naidoo is an Advisor to the Governor of the Reserve Bank in South Africa. He puts it more simply: *'Are they the bigot, or are you?'*

So I went to see Chris Mathias for help, since I knew he always stood up to cultural intolerance when he experienced it himself. His answer? *'This is why people largely stay silent on these issues. They're terrified of being in the firing line.'* Then Chris gave me an example of a rare occasion when he chose to do nothing instead of taking a stand: *'My sister came in from New York with her family and we went out to supper with some friends. There were 12 of us, and eight of the host's party. But when we saw the table, there were only 14 places laid. We all sat down, but the six women from the host's party did not sit; they served. As they served, they were very much part of the group, joining in with the conversations. It didn't feel entirely right, but it felt OK, nuanced. We said nothing, and had a great evening. When does making a stand become intolerance? There isn't an answer.'*

Chris was determined to encourage me: '*As an Indian-born Catholic British guy, this was the call I made. We all make them. We all have our own background in play. Riz is entirely right: there is no cultural neutrality.*'

Jim Sutcliffe summarised all this for me: '*Reuel Khoza is right: you have to stand up, but you have to do it in a culturally intelligent way. My generation does seem to find this difficult, and I'm not sure I can tell you why. Maybe it's just too difficult. If you are a tolerant person, for example, how tolerant should you be of intolerance? It's an impossible question, with no clear answer, but if it's so difficult that you avoid it completely and say nothing, then you end up causing deeper friction, and the issue will just sit there and bother people.*'

I think that this is why an honest book on CQ is needed, which prods us all to respond in our own way. That's what CQ is about.

Why are these prerequisites? Because, without them, the circular nature of CQ learning is interrupted. Let's go back to the paradox. You only develop CQ because people choose to share their ideas, thoughts, theories, stories and aspirations with you, and they will only do it if they think you have enough CQ not to judge, dismiss, ignore or discredit them. As Peter Kulloi says, both seekers and givers are making generous acts. The generosity will not take place unless the seekers have a deep enough interest in people, are honest enough about themselves and are prepared to keep learning and resisting the temptation to demand the solution.

We started with three prerequisites and a possible fourth: standing up to intolerance or ignorance. Before we move on, I'm upgrading the last one to full status as a prerequisite for CQ.

Scenario: University: a perfect CQ learning opportunity

Right now, there are 150 million people in higher education around the world.[2] If, over the next five years, just half of them resisted the temptation to stick with 'people like me' and started learning from the many nationalities and backgrounds that surround them, they would boost their CQ and the world would have millions more bridge-builders. We asked students at universities across the world what it would take to make this happen.

Maria Natasha Tjahjadi – Singapore Management University

In Singapore Management University where I am studying, we get a lot of exchange and international students. What has been done for cultural integration is a buddy system where international students are partnered with locals, or students who have been in Singapore for quite a while.

Another strategy is the 'adopt international students in your group' policy, which is currently done by some of the professors. Basically, in each group there should be at least one international student.

To increase the interaction, you can only come to festivals – such as Halloween or Chinese New Year – if you're partnered with an international student.

There seems also to be a lack of interaction between Singaporeans and local students when we travel abroad. This may be due to too many Singaporeans travelling abroad to the same university at the same time. By encouraging students to go in smaller groups, they will learn more about different cultures and be forced to mix with the local students. Based on my own experience, it will really open up their horizons, making them appreciate diversity more as well as respecting cultural differences.

Vanathy Arul –
University of Wollongong, Dubai

We at University of Wollongong in Dubai are actually trying to achieve the same thing: celebrating cultural diversity and learning from one another. We just recently had our Multi-Cultural Festival, which lasted four days, where students of our university, who hail from different parts of the world, were encouraged to participate and put up stalls that showcased their nations' cultures in terms of clothes, food, music, etc. On the final day, we even had a show where all the participating students danced and sang their traditional songs.

It was a great week! I find that this really helps us learn about other cultures and also, most importantly, interact with people whom we don't otherwise interact with. Events and activities with a balance of fun are the most ideal scenarios for fostering any kind of relationship.

Dalisu Jwara –
Cape Town University, South Africa

Sports get people together, but some sports can be quite good at dividing people too. Sometimes all the players are from one cultural group, but the spectators often are not. Maybe, as well as sports clubs, we should start spectators' clubs. This would bring people together from different cultures.

Du Yanan – Hong Kong University

As Hong Kong is an international metropolis with people from distinctive cultural backgrounds living harmoniously, the University of Hong Kong is open and inclusive with a high level of cultural diversity. However, chances to communicate with foreign peers in class are very limited and superficial. The best would be a friendly 'Where are you from?' And a polite response, with a subtle sense of distance. You may discuss projects throughout the semester, but your understanding about the other's culture remains no deeper than the first impression.

Therefore, I think the most effective way is to blend into each other's daily life. Hong Kong University halls are perfect places for making acquaintances with foreign friends, where you have hall cultural clubs or even foreign roommates.

I think we should suggest to students that they switch homes with a foreign friend for a week or two in the summer or winter vacation. This may be a crazy idea, but I believe it would be an interesting experience.

Volunteers could be recruited who are willing to 'donate their home'. Volunteers' families could be asked to sign up to an agreement and provide evidence for their ability to accept foreign students.

Then the names on the list could be either matched randomly or chosen by the student. For example, Tomoko from Japan could match with Mary from America, and that means Tomoko would spend her summer vacation at Mary's home and Mary at Tomoko's home.

Then the students should meet in pairs and talk with each other about their home, country and traditions they have experienced.

There may be communication problems in non-English-speaking countries and there is the expense of travelling, but as long as we keep a respectful and friendly attitude in mind, we may solve them as the programme operates. Possibly, travel expenses could be supported by cultural foundations? If the programme developed and became as influential as expected, future alumni may donate to keep it operating.

Alice Lang – University of Oxford, UK

I suggest two things: first, I think sport is the best way to meet people from different cultures; it's a great leveller. We are all pursuing the same goals, and we are all shouted at by the coach, regardless of where we come from. Second, the difficulty with universities is that the population is fundamentally a transient one. It isn't easy, therefore, to hook people into local projects when people see themselves as temporary residents. We need to help students to feel invested in the university, and the city.

Disha Sawlani – University of Wollongong, Dubai

My university has students enrolled from about 105 different countries. This means that a vast variety of different cultures are present under the same roof at any given point in time.

There are many ways in which our university contributes to bringing cultural intelligence to its students, starting with the Annual Multi-Cultural Festival. However, in my view, this is not enough for us to understand and respect the cultures altogether. I believe that there needs to be a platform that brings together all these people so that they have a chance to share their opinions and viewpoints about anything and everything.

I have never really thought about this problem in the past, but this challenge got me thinking that we all talk about globalisation and how the world is becoming a smaller place day by day, but when do we ever think about how someone else, who comes from the opposite corner of the world, would deal with a particular situation?

It is still possible to approach students in small numbers and have them share their cultural background and the way of life people lead back in their home countries. This will also give students hands-on experience as to how to deal with people from different societies and give them a sense of how to put their point forward without hurting someone else's feelings.

Clubs and groups are an excellent way of bringing students together and to work in unity towards a common aim and goal. I think we should have a CQ society. This would give students real-life experience of what they are going to be facing in greater magnitude once they graduate.

Michael Yan Shi –
National University of Singapore

NUS has many halls of residence on campus. Each has a distinct group of students. For example, Prince George Park Residence mainly accommodates PhD students from China and India, while Kent Ridge Residence mainly has Singaporean undergraduates. One thing to note is that this phenomenon is not the result of any university rules or policies, but rather has evolved naturally without a clear reason.

My proposal is that for the students who apply to stay on campus, if they can apply to a different residence (instead of continuing to stay in the same residence), they will have higher priority for getting a room. Considering that it is very competitive to get a room on campus, this policy will give students a great motivation to live in another residence and experience a different social and cultural environment.

Zareef Anam –
London School of Economics

Unfortunately, we live in a world where sticking to the 'same herd' comes as a natural instinct and hence external intervention becomes necessary to ensure that different cultures mix.

Universities must place an emphasis on designing coursework that encourages debate and involves working in randomly selected groups over long periods. If the university is multicultural in itself, the group would naturally include a diverse mix of different cultures. Ensuring that the coursework takes place over an extended period would encourage regular interaction between members of different cultures, which is a positive way of spreading cultural intelligence.

Shahbaaz Ali –
Singapore Management University

I think that cultural intelligence is a very vital catalyst to spark off the ideas of tomorrow. We should introduce a module where interested students – from diverse nationalities – should work together with tutors on difficult challenges.

Ridhi Kantelal – University of Oxford, UK

I was born in Portugal. My mother's family is of Indian origin. When I was nine years old, we moved to the US. At 15, we moved to Dubai. In Dubai, I went to a British school where there were lots of Indians and generally more of a mix of nationalities, but something was missing; there was no diversity of culture. People stick to what they know: it wasn't a melting pot, it was more of a platter.

Then I came to Oxford, and this was another huge change. I found British culture tough to adapt to. People were very subtle; I had been used to honesty.

I think you have to celebrate the different cultures more. Things like a Diwali Ball where people can learn about Indian culture, and an International Food Fair where you can try food from all around the world. I have also founded a social enterprise encouraging and assisting Portuguese students to apply and get into Oxford. We organised a Mediterranean party to promote different aspects of the Portuguese culture.

There is a lot of pressure for students to think about their future careers. If I was Vice-Chancellor, I would reduce this pressure and open up lectures and classes to all, so that a maths student could attend a history lecture, for example. Otherwise you create even more divisions.

H.M. Nayef –
University of Wollongong, Dubai

The clubs and activities here at our university are doing amazing work by gathering all the nationalities together, according to common interest. However, you can easily notice that clubs that are based on nationality are the clubs that have the most number of members due to human nature – the tendency of gathering with people similar to us.

I think we should no longer allow clubs based on nationalities. After a while, students will come to realise what they were missing when they stuck to people from the same culture.

Michael Kuwong –
Wits University, South Africa

I am studying for a master's degree in Science in Medicine at Wits University. Originally from Cameroon, I completed my undergraduate degree in veterinary medicine at university in Nigeria. This was my first experience of meeting and interacting with people from all across Africa.

In 2009, I attended a programme run by the University of Illinois which trains vets in terrestrial and aquatic ecosystem health management. The programme takes vets from around the world. We ate, slept and researched together. The programme took place across the United States. We also went to National Parks in Tanzania and conducted aquatic research in Zanzibar.

We all still talk over the phone or on Skype: we are now a family. We learned together what it means to operate globally. The strength of the programme was that it brought together people with common interests and career goals which helped us to bond as a group, but we were from such a range of countries that we were able to learn a lot about other people's worlds.

We all need more opportunities like this, but on our doorstep too.

Yip GuanHui –
National University of Singapore

I study at the National University of Singapore – a university attended by a wide variety of international students, primarily from the Asian region. Anyone who has visited Singapore will observe that we have a rich culinary culture. Food is more than a necessity here; we take pleasure in eating a wide range of culinary delights.

One means of acquiring CQ in my university is to get people of different nationalities and cultures to gather over a good meal. As food is very affordable in Singapore, the university could sponsor the cost of the meal, otherwise the participants could pay a nominal sum towards the cost. We could organise different tables and ensure that there are no cliques – of the same nationalities or cultures – present at the tables. As people are usually reticent, we could ensure that each table is occupied by an even number of individuals so that conversations can occur amongst pairs. Discussion topics could be provided to spark off meaningful conversations.

I've attended such dinner events organised by student groups in Ireland. I think that this is a splendid idea that can be implemented in Singapore too.

---

[1] Denslow, Lanie and Stewart-Allen, Allyson. *Working with Americans*. Harlow: Pearson Education Limited, 2002.

[2] Altbach et al. *Trends in Global Higher Education*.

Part Five

What else does it take? Knowing your Core

Find it

Before embarking on this book, I thought you were more likely to know (or find) your Core if you had a single heritage, deep roots and a settled childhood upbringing, but the more people I have spoken to about CQ, the more I think this assumption was wrong.

As one man in China said to me (and he very specifically asked me not to quote him by name), '*I came from a family where I could not live with my parents. I lived with one family after another, and that meant that I moved from one place to another, and one school to another. If you move around as I did, you become not important. The result is that I was far more free to decide my Core; and the Core which I have developed is entirely mine.*' When I pushed him on what his Core is, he said, '*I have a deep understanding that no one will ever do anything for me except myself.*' I think this includes finding his Core.

Other leaders with a deep Core have clearly spent a long time knitting it together, drawing from the many worlds they know they belong to. I met a young man last week. Now 22, he was born on one continent – of parents from two other and different continents – and educated on yet another. This was followed by the USA for his higher education, and Brazil and Pakistan for his internships. His multiple heritage seems to have resulted in a person who has thought a lot about his Core, recognising the strengths his broad childhood experience has given him in the modern world. His generation does this with much greater ease than mine.

As Shirlene Oh says, '*I came to the UK from Malaysia and spent several years working in China. Many of my generation have crossed the world and then chosen to stay within pockets of their own culture. If you do that, I think it takes two to three generations before you really draw away from the pocket. If you don't, adaptation takes place much quicker. In my case, I adapted quickly – there were no pockets of Malaysians or Chinese where I lived. My children have a dual heritage, which intrigues me. My observations are that they take what they feel fits from each heritage.'*

Riz Ahmed goes even further: '*I was a crazy teenager. I had no idea what my Core was, didn't much care and, if the question raised its head, I would have walked away. I think this meant that I tried lots of things which I might not (and maybe should not) have done. I think the best leaders with CQ are likely to have been all Flex when they were teenagers. Trying everything – no barriers – and discovering what they shouldn't have done. Juggling diametrically opposing values, and learning to really Flex. I think that's how you land on your Core. By the time I started digging in to find it, I had lots of experience to build on. As a result, my Core had been so challenged and pulled about that it ended up much smaller, and perhaps stronger, than many people's. I think I am down to the bare bones now: the stuff I wouldn't change without losing myself completely.'*

Adirupa Sengupta was brought up in Kolkata and, as Chief Executive of Common Purpose Asia-Pacific, is now based in Singapore. She highlighted to me the problem that faces many people in finding Core and Flex when the culture you grow up in does not allow you the freedom to experiment that Riz describes: '*I think some cultures don't allow you to play in Flex as a young person – or even later on. The result is that, as you kick against this lack of freedom, you abandon your culture, and you lose a valuable part of your Core.'*

However, as I talked to more people – young and old, rooted or uprooted, from a single culture or several – more or less the same advice began to emerge about finding your Core, and the values, behaviours, beliefs and habits, large and small, within it. It starts, naturally, with a departure point, your launch pad, and it must be credible to you, and to others.

I discussed this with Reuel Khoza: '*I am a strange mixture of African and a bit of Western, because I was partly educated in Britain. But, at my Core, I am African. If I had used Europe as my point of departure, then I would come across at best as phoney, and at worst as funny.'*

Everyone I spoke to agreed with the need for an authentic starting point. This was their consistent advice on where to go next:

1. Find something you love doing and ask yourself why you love it

I love painting. I love painting only in Scotland, and only if I am painting the sea. I don't love sailing in the sea, but I do love painting it. I have just discovered this in the last six years. I very, very seldom paint, because I am seldom in Scotland (and when I am, there are too many other things to do). But I love it. Why, I ask myself? Because, after five children and a career devoted to Common Purpose, I love doing something that's just for me. I must clarify here that I am a very poor painter: not modesty, just accuracy. No one would ever choose to keep my paintings (other than my family, who want to encourage me), so I can say with total confidence that I do it only for myself.

There's another reason I love painting. Though I loved my father enormously, he instilled in me a feeling that you should do something only if you could excel at it. After many years of taking his advice on all things, I have finally decided that this was inherited Core, which got booted out when I realised it wasn't really mine. Enjoyment is enough, and painting is, in some way, my way of saying this to myself. And, finally, I love trying to paint movement, energy, momentum, dynamism. I paint gulls swooping, clouds exploding, waves crashing and sands shifting, and then all of those blending into each other. What does this tell me? I think my Core is devoted to energy, especially trying to stimulate energy where things have slowed down. I think I have finally discovered that where there is no will to move, there is very little room for me, and I just drive people mad. I discovered this through painting, something I know I love, and know I am not very good at.

2. Go somewhere you don't know and where you won't feel comfortable

As my German colleague Renate Krol tells me, '*You will only really ever find your Core by travelling outside of it.*' Followed by (when she really gets going): '*the best thing you will find in a foreign land is yourself*'. Your frame of reference will be constantly challenged. Your ideas, your assumptions, your manners, your habits, your beliefs, your sense of smell and of space, your mannerisms, your instincts to laugh and cry. Your everything, really. It is daunting for a man and even more daunting for a woman, because the roles of women are so enormously different across the world. As Renate insists: *'Whenever you settle, then you must travel again. Keep experiencing new things and you will expose new things about yourself.'* Your travel could take you to the other side of the world – or to the other side of your own city, because there will be parts of your city that are a completely foreign land to you. Skyscrapers or shacks; boardrooms or holding cells; casualty wards or lecture theatres; performance stages or leaky housing. The more you discover about the world, the more you will discover about what's really in your Core.

Policewoman Ellie Bird agrees: *'Just go. Go on and get out there. Leave what you know for somewhere you don't. And, when you get there, do not treat it like a staging post.'*

Amali de Alwis in Geneva agrees too: *'I hope that my generation will really travel: and not simply stay within the enclave of a sterilised international hotel.'*

I would add this: remember, as we said earlier, that you are travelling to discover the world, not to explain your world to other people (no doubt in the hope that they will think better of it, or even try to emulate it). You're on a mission to learn, not to convert.

Last year, I went on a Common Purpose programme day in Bangalore. That night, in misery and shock, I wrote this blog:

'It's pouring with rain, hammering down, pounding the ground with water, and for the first time in my life, I can't sleep. Last night I spoke at a programme day in Bangalore, India and went with the participants to the slums (Common Purpose can be quite extraordinary). I wonder what it must feel like when the rain thunders on your corrugated roof and the water washes down the gutters around you.

The women were so friendly and delighted to meet us. The children so enchanting, the girls with perfect pigtails (which, after three daughters and many years of practice, I have never mastered). The tiny room was so empty of possessions and so full of people, just three cupboards in the room that had been brought here by the three women as they married into the family. Goats and mud – it has been raining for some time in Bangalore – and more children and dirt all around us. And as you come in, lines of beautifully washed clothes stretched out by the human washing machines that are the women.

I wanted to be friendly – and not intrusive – and interested and to hide my fear of the dirt and the germs and the thought that somehow I might get left behind by my fellow participants. I am so confident at all times that I can cope wherever I find myself, but I had no idea how I would find my way out from here (or who to trust to ask). And in the main road – back up from this side one – the men looked very frightening.

As we leave, an intelligent-looking teenager tries to hijack us toward his house. He seems intelligent, someone in control, like a boy in my son Tom's class in school. He isn't hassling us, just trying to divert us. My fellow participant explains that the boy thinks we are doctors and wants us to help his mother.

So I can't sleep. What's the point of this blog? What's the outcome? After I did my talk earlier, one of the participants used the expression "mass leadership". That's what this will need.'

More 'Flying Dead', I hear you cry, but not if you land properly and fully, and then listen fiercely (I don't mean that you should be fierce, just that your listening should be). The Flying Dead go to new places and look at them through the same – often tired, jet-lagged – eyes.

If you are lucky, and people trust you, and you are slowly developing CQ, you will start to see things through many different eyes, and you'll start to resist the temptation to benchmark it all against the world you know. You can also bring some powerful things back with you.

As Eric Thomas told me: *'Travel makes you reflective about home, and what is special about it, and it gives you things to take home. I brought as Core, back from Australia that social hierarchies in the UK are poisonous and disabling. I have never lost this.'*

Which might explain why, as Vice-Chancellor of Bristol University, he has campaigned so passionately and for so long to increase access to university for young people from UK state schools.

3. Find a story in your heritage and figure out why it has stuck with you

Khadija Rhoda in Johannesburg is very clear about this: *'Find the stories and interpret them for yourself. Don't repeat someone else's version. I love to tell the one about my father, when he started studying at Johannesburg University. He found himself surrounded by Indian Muslims who were racist towards him, because he was Malay Muslim (in those days, described as "coloured"). Day after day, he went to his mentor, crying in desperation, wanting to go home. His mentor told him to carry a box of chocolates. And, every time these people were offensive to him, he should give them a chocolate. My father thought this was the last thing he should do. His mentor told him to "kill them with kindness". He said that it would confuse them and eventually, they would stop abusing him and might even start to respect him. It worked. For my father, it was a lesson in patience, humility and self-restraint.'* Khadija uses this story to help her deal with abuse for marrying someone from a different culture. *'Our version of giving chocolates is to calmly explain why we got married so that people slowly accept it. Eventually. Maybe.'*

It is (now) with enormous embarrassment that I recount a story that is stuck in my heritage. It's the story that goes with a picture that has always hung in the hallway in my family house, wherever we have lived. It's a print of Bolton Square (near Manchester in the North West of England), at the time of the English Civil War. In the middle of the square is a scaffold. The picture shows an ancestor of mine, who volunteered to cut off Lord Derby's head. Months earlier, Lord Derby and his men had ridden through my ancestor's village and killed his wife and all his children. When my ancestor returned from the fields, he had no family. So, when Lord Derby was arrested and brought back to Bolton and they asked for a volunteer executioner, that's why my ancestor stepped forward. What does this say about me, compared with Khadija? Until now, I have thought of the story of my executioner ancestor with pride: he stood up when others wouldn't. It has taken me 55 years, and a very young woman called Khadija, to question this interpretation. Now it tells me that, when you look inside your Core, you don't always find things you like.

Heritage is the reason why Peter Kulloi won't go in the bus lane. He told me it was because of his mother. She was an extraordinary woman, a humble woman who did incredibly brave things. But she had always told him that there was no such thing as 'big brave things', just small ones that sometimes add up to become big and brave. In 1944, she was one of a small group who were given the task of translating the report of what was happening at Auschwitz. It was to be sent to the Governor of Hungary so that he could not claim he did not know what was happening there, and would be forced to act. Aged 24, there she was, sitting on the balcony of a house in Budapest, working on the papers. Mid-sentence, there was a huge gust of wind and the papers blew into the neighbour's garden. The neighbour was a senior officer in the Budapest SS. She didn't run away. Instead, she went to the fence. Where the SS officer picked up the papers without looking at them and handed them back to her.

4. Find moments of stress and unpick them

Robert Care at Arup describes this beautifully: *'Discover what you are willing to do when no one else is watching. What will you do, in the moment? Because stress will push you to your Core and you will find good things in there – and some things that are missing.'*

For me? Hitting my children was something I would never ever do. The only time I have, I remember to this day, as do they. The child I hit, and the children who watched me, were stunned, because this was completely inconsistent with the Core they knew so well. Why did I do it? Because I had told him a hundred times never to rush across a road without looking, and he did it. I was furious; but mostly, I was terrified. Now it makes me realise just how firmly not hitting children is in my Core. Even though I did it – once – it did not (and could never) move to Flex.

Kirsty Bashforth is now Head of Organisational Effectiveness at BP. She recalled for me a moment from early in her career that proved to be pivotal: *'I remember as if it was yesterday an older woman at a party saying to me "Get a skirt, lose the glasses, grow the hair. You look like a lesbian." That was a breakthrough for me – to experience how deeply people's perceptions, assumptions and labels really impact actions. I just laughed.'*

For my banking friend, more recent stress clarified Core: *'The financial crisis has made me understand my Core more. I have always asked myself, what is socially useful banking? The question has become more acute since the financial crisis. I have become more and more clear that only values can really drive value. Some institutions that were worth billions have, overnight, become worth zero. One common factor that killed them was a deficit of values. So, far from making things more confused as some people seem to suggest, the crisis has actually made things much clearer for me. Values matter.'*

5. Keep digging

As you keep working out what's Core, you'll find things you like and things you don't. You will find things you didn't know about, and you'll find that, for every strength you find, there's a weakness you have to recognise and deal with. As Graham Boyce says, *'Every bit of great Core will have a corresponding downside'*. If you are loving to your family, you risk being over-protective. If you take pride in your clarity of thinking as a leader, you are almost certainly sometimes over-simplistic, and so on.

As Reuel Khoza says, *'I am descended from slavery, colonialism and apartheid, and no one will take this from me. It gives me huge strengths – and also weaknesses. It could give me an endless series of excuses too; it's what they call "the African condition", but I refuse to use it in that way. I keep it in my rear-view mirror and keep moving forward.'*

You will also find things you are deeply ashamed of, but which are probably so deeply etched into you that you can only do your best to counterbalance them. I was talking recently to an Indian friend about Core. He described his utter surprise that he could fall in love with someone who was not from India – he had never imagined that this was possible for him. He also knows for certain that he could never have married out of his caste – and is deeply, deeply ashamed of himself for it. Discovering one element that, to his surprise, wasn't in his Core actually clarified one that was: there was another cultural intolerance inside himself that was too deep and embedded to shift.

You will find new things that develop over time. The desire to fight injustice has always been in my Core, but I never had a passion (or possibly even anger) about disability. But some of my children have become disabled in their teenage years, and I have developed a deep commitment to issues about access, health, and long-term care. They now lie firmly in my Core, as a result of experience.

6. Do something you 'don't do'

Just as it's important to go somewhere you don't usually go, I think you have to do something you don't usually do (or even wouldn't have dreamt of doing). Now in his fifties, Peter Kulloi says, *'Our generation had to decide what it was going to know at too young an age. Decide to study something very new. It is good to go back and learn more. It reminds you how little you know, and excites you about how much more you could know.'*

Jude Kelly puts it even more simply: *'Next time someone hands you a baby, take it. Don't say "I'm not good with babies" and fold your arms. When you hold a baby, somehow you feel your Core.'*

I put Jude's suggestion to my banking friend. Is it a good test of Core? *'I like holding babies and I agree that there is something very elemental about it. I think it pushes you to understand how you relate to young people. But what I found fascinating when I heard Jude's words is that she uttered them at all. The words "hold a baby". They made me feel very uncomfortable. My immediate response was: are these words appropriate in a discussion about leadership? They are evocative and emotional; it felt to me that they didn't fit here. Then again, they made the point very powerfully. It made me think about how I communicate, whether I am becoming narrow myself. I won't forget them and – above all – I won't forget my own response to them.'*

As an expert in risk management, he had his own powerful example: *'Only to do things which you like or are comfortable with is by far the most dangerous thing you could do, because the things that make you grow are the things you have never done before. One of my greatest learning experiences was the three and a half years I spent in Saudi Arabia with my family and my job. When I moved to Saudi, several people – the vast majority – told me not to go. They warned me that the environment would be hostile to my Christian faith. When I got there, initially I thought I had landed on Mars. Yet, at the end of our time there, it was, and still is, one of the richest learning experiences in our entire lives.*

Being in Saudi Arabia did more to reinforce our core values, in ways which one would not have envisaged initially. Being in a society that defines itself by its faith (the head of state's title is Custodian of the Holy Mosques first, and then King, in that order of priority) challenged me to think through what it means to prioritise faith in a society, and in my life. Living among a society where everything stopped during the five prayer times a day challenged me on my own beliefs of the centrality of prayer. Being woken each morning by the call to prayer was a wake-up call in more ways than one, and discovering the richness of Islamic culture, with its role in the creation of algebra, was part of my continuing education. The experience had other dimensions. In a society with no cinemas and pubs to go to, it meant that socialising focused on relationships with people. The whole experience made it very clear to me that relationships – with people and with God – were what made up my Core and what are really important. In the strangest of ways, looking back, I don't think I could have made it through the last few years of the financial crisis without this learning and my experiences in Saudi Arabia. It's important to add that the whole experience reaffirmed my faith and gave me insights into how one personally gains a sense of freedom rather than fear. It is important that people live without fear. Fear tends to close us down and makes us less than ourselves. The only person one should fear is God.'

For Issa Baluch, from Dubai and now at Harvard, religious faith revealed Core in a different way: *'I am a Muslim, and the Muslim faith does not permit adoption. My wife is Christian. Deep in her Core was the wish to adopt. So I trusted her Core, and did it to make her happy, and to save another soul. We have had four children and adopted four more, and the experience has enriched my life. With one of our adopted children, we had to appear before the Nairobi Family Court (not that it is a family court; we were in there with many criminals too). When the judge looked at us all – at me, my wife and my kids – he said, "This adoption cannot happen. Ms Baluch is white, Mr Baluch is brown. The other children are of many colours. And this child is black." Fortunately, we had a very good lawyer who made our case well. We pushed back, and were approved. I left thinking about that judge, who saw nothing but colour. It really doesn't matter: we are us, the Baluch family, and we have built our own culture.'*

All these stories are personal and emotional examples of doing the unfamiliar. Jim Sutcliffe gives me an example of how it can have value at the corporate level too: *'Social media have changed the way companies deal with their customers. You can't say that you prefer your own corporate culture, and don't like all this tweeting stuff, for example. You have to learn to live with it. I am on the board of a company and, one day, we arranged for all of us to tweet over one whole day of meetings, just to understand how it worked. At first, we were all pretty polite, but it did not take long before we started tweeting each other about the quality of the presentation we were seeing. We were sending each other messages about the talk, while the poor speaker had no idea what was going on. Then we all looked at how tweets were changing patterns of behaviour. How communities now form in new ways. How some tweeters have even managed to get company logos on their tweets. It made us all realise how silly it was to think that you could ever suppress it, or "manage" it from the boardroom. The trouble is that most large corporations are about control. Most CEOs get upset if they don't feel in control. Social media means that they can now be upset most of the time.'*

So do something you don't do, because you'll learn something interesting. Though, even here, there are lines you probably have to draw for yourself. Peter Kulloi has done all kinds of things in his career, from negotiating huge deals in New York to starting a camp in Hungary for children with serious illnesses, but there's one thing he won't do: *'A friend invited me to a tango lesson. I am not a dancer, and I just couldn't convince myself to do it. I would feel so stupid.'*

7. Work out clashes in Core

Sometimes you hit a situation when two bits of your Core compete head-on. Both are important to you, but only one can win. Working out how – and why – you resolved the clash can be unsettling, but helpful.

Maria Figueroa Kupcu's experience in New York took me back 20 years to when I felt the same clashes myself: *'Sure, I have clashes in my Core. I am ambitious, and want to have an impact in the world. This means that I am often not home until 7pm, and the kids need to eat at 5pm. How can I possibly be a decent mother, if I do not cook for my children? This is deep in my Core, and my Italian roots. How can I show my love? How can I pass on my cultural heritage? How can I nourish my kids, physically and emotionally, if I don't eat with them? And, on top of this, my kids don't speak Italian. We have been outpaced by America: they only speak English.'*

I have a very successful black friend whose surname happens to be Smith. As he tells me, with a smile, *'I did not know my father. All he ever gave me was the name Smith. But it is a name that has allowed me to walk through many doors before anyone realised who I am.'*

For him, the clash in Core is violent – and partly historical: *'One of the most interesting experiences in my life is my journey to becoming British, alongside being Barbadian. The journey, being a child of the Commonwealth, is a complex journey, but one which one must take. My roots and heritage in the Caribbean and Barbados are very important. It is not an exaggeration to state that, over the last 50 years, one of the best places to have grown up and had your formative years as a black person anywhere in the world would be Barbados. Similarly, if you look dispassionately and objectively at it, I think London is one of the best places to be black in the modern world. This duality of experience is increasingly common around the world. I'm reminded of it every day. I work in Canary Wharf, quite close to West India Quay. It is called "West India Quay" not because the Docklands is palm-fringed, but rather because, when it was set up, the Docklands was part of the triangular trade critical to Britain's development, of which the West Indies was also a central part. And therein rests the complexity. It is almost certain that some of those ships that came into the Docklands came from the West Indies (hence West India Quay) and bore slaves, possibly my ancestors or the ancestors of friends. We were the cargo that was traded. Less than 200 years on since the abolition of slavery, it is remarkable that Britain and the Docklands, and indeed Barbados, exist in a very different world.'*

Of course, the clashes aren't always in your own Core. Sometimes, as we explored earlier in the book, your Core bumps into someone else's, and sometimes yours can clash with an entire roomful of other people's. Here is an example of when that happened to me.

A few years ago, I was asked to speak about global leadership at the Judge Business School in Cambridge. It was a major conference, with an audience full of female leaders from all around the world. That day, I was travelling back from the US, so I knew the connections would be tight, but it looked just about doable, so I accepted. On the day, I just made the last possible train at Liverpool Street Station. But, as I ran along the platform, I tripped and fell badly on my knee. There was no blood, but I was left with one ripped trouser leg and a badly bruised knee. I climbed on to the train, swallowed, tidied myself up and tried to concentrate on what I would be saying.

When I arrived in Cambridge, I hobbled straight to the college and on to the platform. The audience of beautifully presented women stared at me. I made a joke about my stressful trip and launched into my talk. Halfway through it, I just stopped, in mid-sentence. I said that I was not sure I should continue, because I was not convinced that anyone was doing anything but looking at my torn trouser leg. You could have heard a pin drop. I said to them, '*I accept that many of you must feel that after my fall, I should have pulled out of this talk, since I didn't have time to find another pair of trousers. But I would just like to say that if I say I will speak at an event, I will not let anyone down. I will be there, come what may. This is deep in my Core. For you, it is clearly disrespectful to turn up with ripped trousers; to me, it is a sign of deep respect that I would make it, come hell or high water.'*

What followed is one of the most interesting sessions about global women's leadership I have ever had the honour to be involved in. We talked about how the path I had chosen would have ended careers in some countries, in the Arab world and the US, most notably. About how far you should go to be you. About clashing Cores, and whether I should have Flexed for them. We even discussed whether I should have just ignored the blank faces in the room and kept on speaking. And then we talked about how powerful a common Core can be in a room faced with one individual who had a different one, since they had all sat and judged as a group, not listening to a word I said.

True to form with CQ, there was no single answer. There were multiple ones, depending on different Cores. But I certainly learnt about how deeply important presentation is for some people and in some cultures, and they learnt about the power of groups to judge collectively rather than individually. How easy it is for an individual to feel bullied, even if nothing is said, and the possibility that an act they saw as beyond the pale might just have a different Core behind it.

8. Go to the place that best connects you with your Core

For some people, place matters enormously. A place that gives you peace, or the opposite: a place that stimulates you and helps you connect to what is Core for you.

I have a place that does this for me. It's full of trees, trees that are hundreds of years older than me and will be there, I hope, for many more. It's where, under one cherry tree, one summer, we brought my youngest son Tom home to meet his four siblings in the August sun. It's a place that, for me, heals and inspires and strengthens, but I know that I am lucky.

Not having a place is revealing too. Reuel Khoza doesn't: *'I refuse to be defined by geography where my Core is concerned. It's restricting. Apartheid South Africa tended to do this. Johannesburg is where you went and became a migrant. Your homeland was where someone else had settled you. I loathe that expression in the housing world, "we will house them". I have now bought a farm near my place of birth and I go there for reflection, but not for Core. Of course, Mandela said that a cell is also a great place for reflection.'*

9. Establish your own stories

Heritage stories are important, but you shouldn't live there. Michael Hastings put this very well to me: *'I like Reuel Khoza's expression "rear-view mirror", I like it a lot. So, in the main, I am looking forward. The past may well be important, but it is the past. As a black man in my 50s, I think young black people should do more to frame themselves in the future than the past. I think Black History Week was good in its time, but now we should move on. Stop obsessing about maintaining something from the past, and start claiming the future. It's only the rear-view mirror: you can't drive without it, but mainly you should be looking where you're going.'*

Your own story is just as important. The parts of your own narrative that define who you are and what is Core for you now. Reuel Khoza has a story that has carried him forward all his life: *'I was an activist at university. Then I became a research-officer-cum-junior-lecturer at that university. My mother and father were delighted and proud. Then I got fired, for being a political activist. I went home, desperate at the thought of how deeply disappointed my father would be. He wasn't. He simply said, "I know you will bounce back." This has sustained me throughout my adult life. It's deeply etched in my Core; I know that I always will bounce back.'*

Sometimes, your own story will also reveal things that can move to Flex. Chris Mathias gives a good example: *'I used to believe that no one had the right to tell me to do something, without the corresponding requirement to tell me why. I then had the right to accept their explanation, or not. This was etched into me: I was actually expelled from school for it. I think I was the first boy to be expelled for 300 years. They said it was for "subversive and seditious behaviour". The headmaster told me what to do, I asked why, he told me to just do it, so I said that I wouldn't. In fact, I think I said that I would only accept this answer if he was God. So I was expelled. I still feel like this, but it is no longer in my Core. I am older and wiser and less confrontational, less stroppy. I am willing to accept that, if it is someone I trust, then they can ask me without having to give me an explanation. I am still likely to ask why, of course!'*

Of course, you can also create your own story, for the future. Which is exactly what a young Lebanese friend is doing: *'In terms of the most notable action I have taken in response to cultural intolerance, I would say that my wedding constitutes that action. Marrying an atheist of Muslim background was an enormous pill to swallow for my Christian family, who are heavily scarred by the Lebanese civil war and retain fears about Muslims. My husband and I had a civil wedding in London and could have stopped there: appeasing our families with an inoffensive Western approach to marriage. But neither of us felt that a civil wedding alone reflected the wealth of our backgrounds, or the decision we were taking together. Instead, we decided to celebrate both cultures – Pakistani and Lebanese – fully and to invite (that is, oblige) our families – with all their baggage, biases and preconceived notions – to experience both wedding ceremonies fully. I brought my Lebanese Christian family and friends to Pakistan, and my husband's Pakistani family came to Lebanon.*

Today, when you ask my parents about Pakistan, they speak proudly about it. Forever, they will carry the generosity, love, colour and joy they experienced there. Through real experience, their perspective has changed.'

10. Keep looking outwards

My Barbados-born friend gave me a very nice example of this: '*There are times when I really have to check myself so that I don't slide too far back into Core. All kinds of strange things make you know you are in Core. Food does it for me. I know that I should have food in Flex, but it isn't. I go to the same restaurants and I prepare the same recipes, with fish and peppers and spices and cassava. I think it is almost a default position to go for experiences that give you comfort, or that you have already experienced. I associate food with my childhood, my heritage and the sense of growing up. My wife is always pushing me to go to new restaurants. I really think I should stop resisting so much.*'

Recently, I talked to a young man who was very taken with Riz's idea that having very little Core as a teenager could be an advantage or a strength. He started to draw a curve for me, to represent the size of your Core over a lifetime. He started the curve high on the page because, as a young person, you often adopt your parents' Core. Then, as you shed the Core you inherited, the curve dives down through the teenage years and then starts to climb again. The older you get, the higher it goes.

I must say, it didn't do it for me. In fact, no curve would. I think the size of your Core is far too individual. Indeed, for many people, as we saw earlier, the Core actually gets smaller over time. That can be a very good thing, but it can also become a problem. Where his ever-rising age curve did resonate with me is my fear that age brings a temptation to get more impatient and less tolerant of the unfamiliar. To prefer your own company, or the company of old friends. To cling more to the world you know, and engage less with the world that surrounds you.

How often do you hear of older people who remained deeply engaged with people from other generations and cultures well into their old age? I think this is probably only ever mentioned because it is the exception rather than the rule.

I hope that friends will tell me if my curve does start to climb and more and more becomes Core as I engage less and Flex less, with fewer people.

Reveal it

Some leaders have a deep Core. But, precisely because it is deep and personal (and perhaps slightly embarrassing), they have a real unwillingness to reveal it. For some, it would feel too self-centred to talk about yourself, to reveal your Core, which would probably involve talking about your beliefs or family or roots. For them, the line of what is unprofessional is drawn somewhere here. Though this may all be perfectly sensible, I think it is not an option for a leader in search of CQ, for a number of reasons:

- because you develop CQ largely through others who choose to reveal themselves to you. It is a two-way process, and if you will not reveal much, neither will they.

- because generosity is a crucial part of CQ. Generosity of spirit seems to be something that crosses all boundaries. Kingsley Wheaton, Director of Corporate and Regulatory Affairs at British American Tobacco, agrees: '*A key trait in people we relate to, and therefore of leadership, is often generosity of spirit. It does not need translating. You have to be generous with whatever it is that you have: money, yourself, your knowledge, your story, your time. Listen to people – that is a generous act. You remember people who generously helped you to navigate something.*'

- because, if you don't, people will think that you think you're above them. Genevieve Barr, who runs our programme for disabled students, tells me, '*We once had a speaker who did not really answer any of the questions people asked her. Each time she was asked a question, she used a quote, or told a story about something a colleague did, or quoted something that happened in ancient Greece. There was nothing wrong with what she said, but the group was trying to connect with her personally: as an experienced senior leader who had made a difference. Everything she said was interesting, but she gave no personal insight. We didn't learn anything about her and what she had done. It came across as arrogance: that she was "too senior" to share personal insights. But, if you want to engage with an audience – especially a diverse audience – I think you need to put yourself out there, flawed or otherwise (but ideally flawed). That's how you get people to identify with you.'*

- and lastly because if you don't reveal your Core, people will start to believe you don't have one, and with that, comes a lack of trust.

The moment to reveal Core may come naturally, but it may also have to be prompted. Leaders run team meetings and stakeholder events to get people out of a work context so that a deeper understanding and trust can develop. Common Purpose is increasingly taking teams out into their cities – or the cities they are meeting in for a conference or strategy meeting – to understand it, but also to understand each other by doing something entirely different together.

Sometimes you have to create a situation in which you can reveal your Core to people if they are to trust you. I watched a colleague do this last month. Alison Coburn knew that she needed to get a very difficult group of stakeholders onside. She knew that their default position was to say no. She also knew that they seldom dealt with Western women, so the default position seemed even more likely to be the outcome. I saw her weave the conversation to a place where she spoke about her own family and childhood, and the message came across loud and clear that Alison would never impose a solution on anyone. It was clear to them that if they said no, Alison would leave and 'go home', respecting their view. I suspect that they were so used to people talking and talking and revealing nothing that when, in all the noise, something genuine (that revealed Alison's Core) came through, it was loudly heard. They acted on it and decided to go with her ideas.

Amali de Alwis tells me that something a bit like this happened recently in Geneva. A senior global director was talking about the need for more leadership in a sector. At one point, rather than referring to a CEO as 'he', he very elegantly slipped in the word 'she'. Amali says she was watching carefully, and she caught something in his voice and eyes that convinced her that he had done it deliberately. Amali also says that such an act can genuinely surprise you. She admits that, before this moment, she would not have expected this of the man in question: *'I was surprised and delighted. I think some people forget what a small act like that means to people. If you comment back – as I did – they seem almost surprised that you heard it.'*

So you must reveal Core – the outcome can sometimes be even better than you anticipated. But doing it is not easy for people who are private, or quiet, or modest. Sometimes, for them, it is only when things get really difficult or contentious that they reveal their Core. And then it bursts out because they are irate (or even offended). Then you sit back and listen hard. Because Core is being revealed and may not be again for some time!

Unless, of course, you have found cultural intolerance in your Core. Then it is better not to reveal it. (More on this later.)

And stick to it

So, let's assume that you've wrestled with what's really Core for you, and you've come to some conclusions (at least for now). You've managed to overcome the temptation to keep it to yourself and decided that it's better to reveal it to other people. Pretty quickly, as a leader, you'll run into another problem: staying true to it, especially in situations where it would be much more comfortable not to, with people who would much prefer you to accept the status quo and Flex away merrily, with nothing ever being challenged or changed.

Sometimes, Ellie Bird tells me, being consistent with your Core is very tough, and there can be a price to pay: *'I have policed many major British cities now. I find it impossible to ignore things. But, if you question things like the sectarianism in a city, if you ask, for example, "Why do the songs on the street refer back to battles no one remembers?" you get any of the following replies:*

"Yeah, right, it's been like this for centuries, what are you going to do about it?",
or "As an outsider, how dare you . . . ?", or even "What are you talking about?"
Eventually, you become desensitised to it. But just accepting it as the norm
doesn't fit with my Core. You can't Flex on this kind of stuff: you have to stand
up and name it, and all the more so if it's not your battle. You won't get a round
of applause for it, but, as a leader, if that's what you want, you took the wrong
route. If not turning a blind eye is at your Core, then there is no option. However
unpopular you are, or however career-limiting it becomes.'

People tell me that, in the 'old days', you could abandon your Core for
a while, as you travelled to faraway places. Even if you can live with
yourself, I believe this is no longer an option. There is no 'abroad' any
more. The world is too small: you will come across fellow travellers
wherever you go, and the digital world is even smaller. The Internet very
quickly reveals variations or inconsistency in Core.

But what happens if you do?

I spoke to Robert Care from Arup. It's a fascinating company whose
Danish founder had a deep Core and did all he possibly could to trans-
fer it into the great company he had started. Robert showed me a copy
of a speech that Ove Arup, then 74, gave in 1970 to his management
colleagues at the now-multinational company. Entitled 'The Key
Speech', it aimed to set out his view of the values of the company and
his vision for how his colleagues might grow it without losing what
made the company so good.

It's a very good speech (indeed, I believe that the company still gives
a copy of it to each new member of staff when they join), and it sets
a very high bar, both personally and professionally. I asked Robert
how he, or any of his colleagues, could ever hope to live up to it. He
laughed and said, *'Sometimes, when you make a decision and then read the*
piece and think you have failed, the real test – the really crucial one – is what
you do next.'

Ove Arup's speech also includes the line *'the man who bangs his head*
against the wall could learn from the reed that bends in the wind'. You have to
Flex too, but he sets this against a background of deep principles. For a
leader, Core means something only if it very seldom moves, and Flex
means a lot more when it isn't all you have to offer.

As Mike Brearley puts it, '*Some captains lead by being with their men and their teams all the time, and I think they begin to lose a sense of themselves.*'

To summarise on Core. If you want to discover CQ, you will:

- work hard to find your own Core;
- stick to it;
- take care over the small things in your Core as well as the big things;
- keep it under constant review, adding (and weeding) regularly;
- resist the ageing effect;
- counterbalance the bits you're ashamed of;
- watch out for cultural intolerance;
- accept that you are not the norm against which all else is judged;
- allow others to have their own, different Cores;
- make sure it's your Core, and not just inherited, or imposed, or adopted;
- reveal it, and share it;
- give it a good airing every now and then;
- recognise how important Flex is too.

But before we charge on, secure in the knowledge that Core is what we have to pin down and then we can move on to Flex, it is worth standing back to remember what a nightmare this can all be for many people.

I sat with a young British/Turkish friend of mine in the spring. She is a newly qualified NHS doctor, working long shifts in a busy East Midlands hospital. Born in Britain to Turkish parents, she is a mixture of confidence and lack of it. In her Core, there is both a strong cultural and family tie that binds her to Turkish tradition and a powerful sense of individual freedom that comes from growing up in Britain.

For her, these Core elements come into stark contrast as she considers who she is going to marry. She tells me that he will have to be a Turk, and a Turk from the village her parents came from. Why? *'Because, that way, we will know his family and background. We will have a common culture, dancing, foods and dialect. Both families will have the same expectations of a new bride, and they will share how they practise religion.'* I asked about dancing. She tells me that they will know when and how to dance at the wedding. For example, her family would never dance Halay, which comes from Eastern Turkey. Theirs is Zeybek dancing, a completely different style.

As for 'expectations of a new bride', she explains that she will be expected to help with cooking and cleaning, without being asked. She must show respect to her elders, though she thinks that they won't be as strict as in the eastern part of Turkey, where a daughter-in-law would be expected to wear a headscarf, could never show the soles of her feet to an elder and must look down at the floor at all times.

On religion, she says that by sticking to 'her village', they would avoid someone too religious, which she and her family would see as backward, requiring her to fast, and pray five times a day. And dialect? Simple: dialects in other parts of Turkey use the same words, but the accent and the slang are so different that you can't understand them.

My friend thinks that if push came to shove, her parents would be OK about a Turkish husband who came from another village, but he would have to tick all the other boxes. He must also have a job of appropriate status and be well educated.

She has been brought up to be a good candidate as a wife, and she knows that she must not compromise this and that if she does, people will gossip: *'One step out of line and someone will notice. You will bring shame for the family and you will lose your perfect candidate status.'*

The problem is that there is something too British instilled in her to be able to do the normal Turkish thing: *'I want to make decisions. I want to be equal, not secondary. I want to get control of my life, not let someone else do it. I don't mind making compromises, but I want to be heard.'*

The week before we spoke, she was due to meet a well-qualified candidate. He arrived in London just as she was about to fly out on holiday, having done a long shift at the hospital. He more or less instructed her to come and meet him. She said no and explained. He replied that she could sleep on the plane. She didn't go: '*I don't want him to think that he has that kind of power. There is a way to persuade me, and that's not it. If I say no, I mean no.*' As the British bit of her Core came to the surface, she smiled: '*I have trained for years to be a doctor, and lived at home. I can't wait to get my own salary, so that I can start an independent life.*' But it won't be easy: '*I love my culture, and I'm worried about losing it if I let someone else in. I will end up getting more involved in their culture, and less in mine. I know that my Turkish Core is best; it has taught me morals and the importance of family. Family comes first in anything and everything.*'

She tells me that her brother has made a break, and is now experiencing what it is like to live without your parents defining you when you come home every day. He is now happy – but he doesn't know how to make his parents happy. Where to, then, I ask. '*Maybe I should just wear a headscarf. That would send a "go away" message to all non-Turkish men.*' But right away she adds, '*Then again, I don't want to limit who I associate with.*'

Torn between two strong parts of her Core, she is horrified by the idea of not being accepted, and fears ending up in limbo: '*I am terrified of being judged, and failing. I have to be liked. If someone doesn't like me and I don't understand why, I get very upset. I think about it for days. That's why I avoid people outside work.*'

Just to be clear: I am writing this book as if this were all simple stuff. Some of it is, but a lot of it isn't. It is very difficult. I think you have to keep firmly in mind how hard it can sometimes be to stick to your Core when, all around you, others are losing theirs (and questioning yours).

I think you have to sit down sometimes with someone who is very different from you and just listen.

Calibrating your Flex

I thought that I would try to unpick the five areas of Flex that people I have met seem to struggle with most, sometimes because they are the most common problems; sometimes because they are the most tricky. They are:

- using language (and particularly English);

- dressing and greeting;

- whether humour helps or hinders;

- adapting to local ways;

- understanding pride (or 'face').

No doubt there will be plenty more areas of Flex to unpick, but I have chosen these five to start with (I hope that you will tell me the ones I have missed.) On all five, you have to calibrate your Flex, and there are no single (or even lasting) answers. By definition, there can't be: after all, we are in Flex.

Language matters

Language is an enormous barrier to CQ. Consider the languages of the generations: expressions that come in and out of usage, adopted by young people or remembered by old, and often dividing the two.

Consider the jargon of the sectors, designed to keep them apart (and pretty effective at it). And, in each case, keeping outsiders out. The 'win, win, win' expression keeps East and West apart – and it keeps the private and NGO sectors apart too. How often have I heard NGO leaders muttering about private-sector leaders *who can turn anything into a competition*? Or private-sector leaders tearing their hair out at the *waffle words in the NGO sector*? Sometimes it is almost as if language is being used to set traps to catch people out: to make them misunderstand, or say the wrong thing. A colleague joined the police recently and she spent most of her first year acquiring a new lexicon: *There is a whole language of made-up words which only exist in policing,* she tells me.

We all have our private languages, but leaders in search of CQ need to be very careful when and how (and with whom) they use them.

At least the widespread use of English has made communicating across cultures much easier. English now has official or special status in at least 75 countries, with a total population of over two billion. This is undoubtedly helpful in many ways. Increasingly, people the world over can slip into a common language and communicate. This has a huge impact on levels of trust and of CQ. Parents in many parts of the world today will go hungry to pay for their children to learn to speak English and make the resulting jump in their prospects.

Though this 'common language' makes CQ much easier at one level, I do fear that it makes it far more difficult at another. In a growing number of countries, the majority of people are communicating through their second language (with South Africa and India being at the forefront). The downside of this is that ideas sometimes get lost, misunderstandings flourish and endure, words get longer (and sentences with them) and meanings get missed.

The dominance of English also presents a particular problem for leaders whose first language is English, because there is a high probability that it is also their only language, and this can be a huge weakness. In the summer, I met the Chairman of a large company that has global aspirations. I asked him how many languages were spoken on his board. He smiled confidently and said, 'four'. I thought for a moment and looked at the list. Then I asked what would happen if you didn't count the Dutchman (since the Dutch tend to speak multiple languages). How many languages would the board members speak then? He paused, and said 'one'.

So many leaders whose first language is English do not learn a second one. But does this matter, if theirs is the dominant language? I think it does; it matters a lot. For several reasons.

To start with, they never experience at first hand the deep frustration, the awkward, tongue-twisting agony of attempting to get across your ideas which are flowing at 100 miles per hour, while your tongue and your poor brain (and whatever connects them) are stuttering and spluttering along at 10 miles an hour; of trying to communicate in a different language. Or if they do, it is only briefly, and abandoned pretty rapidly. English-only speakers never really grasp that, as a result, their communication with huge parts of the world is suboptimal. If you talk to university students who only speak English (who will tell you at length how global they aspire to be) and you ask them why they spend so little time with foreign students, they too often reply, *'You know, their English isn't that good.'*

The second problem is that people who only speak English don't understand just how complex and nuanced translation can be and how vulnerable it is to misinterpretation. As a French speaker, I sometimes get asked for translations. Transactional, simple translations. Actually, they're not even translations. Often, I am asked for exact equivalents: '*What is the precise word in French for . . . ?*' And, when you stumble to formulate a sensible answer, it's you who seems to be the stupid one, and not them for asking a stupid question. I spoke in France at a leadership conference some years ago, just after an English speaker. He did a great talk – except that his refrain was a call for more collaborative leadership. I slipped him a note at a break saying that collaboration had a slightly different connotation in France, *collaborateurs* having been the traitors in World War Two. His response – scrawled across my note, which I have kept – read, '*They should learn English.*'

The third reason is that, all too often, English-only speakers think that if the other person speaks English too, then they share more than just a language. As Eric Thomas says, '*English is only a language: it is not a culture.*'

Kuben Naidoo in South Africa agrees: '*The greatest danger of the widespread speaking of English is that people start to think that, if they are all using one language, then it must be one culture.*'

And it can get you into real problems: '*If you go to parts of English-speaking Africa and call your managers together to brief them, they will probably say "yes, yes, yes" to everything. Then you will leave, and nothing will happen. When you go back and ask, "So why did you say yes, yes, yes?" they will say, "Because it is our culture to say yes to bosses."*'

As an ambassador, Graham Boyce has seen so many English speakers fall into the same trap: '*Even the simplest of language can be baffling. In my experience, for example, Arabs will very seldom say no. But they won't say yes either.*' And the British can be the worst of the English speakers, with all that understatement: '*It endlessly gets the British into trouble. Try to sell something to a German and they will maybe say, "No, I don't want to buy." Do the same to a British person and they will say, "On the whole, I would rather not." Now, tell me, is that a yes or a no?*'

So, despite being masters of the most powerful language in the world (at least for now) – and with all the advantages this brings with it –

English-only speakers start their CQ journey at a considerable disadvantage. And, understandably, they often believe the opposite.

At the same time, English itself is evolving. Common Purpose in India is a separate organisation, with its own Indian board, operating under licence from the global Common Purpose Charitable Trust. When the Indian company changed its accountants to use a local Indian firm, I remember receiving the first management report from them. I read it and re-read it, wondering if the author had been educated at all. There was a whole strange set of words there, some familiar, some unfamiliar and some halfway between the two. My Indian colleagues told me to think again, and that this unusual language was Hinglish: '*Get over it. After all, we are the new owners of English. There are many more English speakers in India than there are across the rest of the world.*' They told me to adapt: '*The English language is alive and evolving and Flexing. Make sure you Flex too.*'

At the time, I was wrestling particularly with a half-familiar and half-unfamiliar word: 'prepone'. They had asked me to '*prepone a meeting*'. I queried it, and they came straight back with: '*Julia, if you can postpone a meeting, why can't you prepone it? We want you to move it forward, because otherwise not all of us can make it.*' Fair point, and logical Latin. So I preponed it.

As I write now, my computer is flashing that I should spellcheck the words 'Hinglish' and 'prepone' above, but I suspect that this won't be the case for much longer. With language, Microsoft Word shows that it can Flex too. If you look on Indian mobile phones, 'Hinglish' appears on the language drop-down menu. I suspect that before too long, 'prepone' won't have lots of red dots highlighting it either.

Dalisu Jwara in South Africa tells me that it is not just about language and vocabulary either. Accents are important too: '*At Cape Town University, we are very intolerant as students. We had a lecturer who was intelligent, but not eloquent. He was from Lesotho. People treated him very badly. They did not listen to what he was saying – they only heard how he was saying it. His accent was very thick. They complained to his face, and on Facebook. And, while he was lecturing, they held separate – often loud – conversations with each other. I have seen this happen more than once. People discriminating against thick accents. Deciding that they will only listen to people who sound like them. I heard*

an amazing lecturer on quantitative economics last week. His ideas were power-
ful, but my fellow students only heard a thick Zimbabwean accent, and not for
long, because they walked out of the lecture early on.'

I met a fascinating woman on a flight to Berlin recently. She was one of
the leading voice coaches for film stars. I asked her about accents. She
said, *'Mostly, these days, I coach tunes. Not words or even pronunciation, but*
tunes. Get the tune to a voice wrong, and people will not trust it. In the past, it
might have been about grammar, but that is not what people hear any more.'

A very good friend from my student days belongs to many different
countries. She was born in the USA, to Welsh and German parents,
who met as Marshall Scholars after World War Two. I sometimes hear
her on the phone talking to her mother in Wales. She is speaking in
English – but with an entirely different sound from her normal speaking voice. She tells me, *'When I move to a Welsh tune in my voice, people*
tend to assume that I am putting it on, or worse, mocking it.' (I have to admit
to being one of these people for many years.) *'But I am not even conscious*
of it. It's just that I am clicking into another world and means of communicat-
ing. Language isn't just words; it's poetry and music too.' And, when she
spoke to her father, she did the same – but German this time. Not
German words, or even German pronunciation, but a German tune.
She tells me that if I spoke German, I would appreciate which tune she
was using: *'The tunes have very different meanings in Germany. In fact,*
listening to the tunes of post-unification Germany was fascinating. If you
sounded like you came from Saxony, you were associated with the quaint old
pre-war films – and largely not listened to.' Then she adds, *'I think sometimes*
we think of this as prejudice, but it's not that deep really. It's just stuff – Core
and Flex – that needs reframing.'

Which brings us back to 'cultural stuckness'. Tell them to travel.

On the plane to Berlin, my fellow traveller pronounced Henry Higgins
dead – and the world he lived in too. She explained: *'You know the Henry*
Higgins trick? In My Fair Lady, *when Zoltan Karpathy guesses the heritage of*
the voice-coached heroine Eliza Doolittle? It's very difficult to do nowadays.
There are only a few entirely ghettoised cultures, and languages, left. Voices have
been exposed to one another the world over, and, in the great melting pot of
sounds, they are blending and merging.'

I asked her whether she thought that language should lie in Flex. After all, many people are very clear that their language is an essential part of their culture. If their language is lost, their culture will be too. Is it right to fear the globalisation of the English language? Interestingly, she predicted that things would soon be going back in the other direction: *'We are in a transition moment now anyway. As English starts to dominate, people are starting to privatise their English. English is starting to splinter into many versions: Hinglish, Chinglish, Singlish. Different words are starting to have different meanings, with different stories behind them. Before you know it, we won't know what each other is talking about again.'*

But would this be so new for English anyway? English has always been the ultimate hybrid language, taking influence from the Vikings, Romans and Normans, through invasion, pre-1066; from the Renaissance, and the expansion of trade; and from every country of the Commonwealth (and more) ever since then. And it's telling that English doesn't have a body to 'protect its purity'. Like CQ, its messy openness to difference has always been its strength. (Here, of course, I am deliberately ignoring the mutterings of people like my husband, who have a habit of reminding me about proper spellings and usages.) English is full of 'mistakes' that have stuck. Not that English speakers shouldn't be careful, and sensitive, in the way they use it. But they start with a very elastic language (unlike Latin, the last international 'lingua franca', if you were privileged enough to learn it). And, right now, it is stretching in some very interesting directions.

But one thing is very clear in my mind: leaders with CQ keep most language in Flex. They don't complain when they have to adapt expressions or words. Even their favourite ones, if they find that they are received differently from the way they were meant. And – crucially – I think leaders with CQ allow other people to decide exactly which words to use to describe themselves. Over the years I have been told, by black people, to describe black people in many different ways. This seems to me to be wholly reasonable. And I struggle, for example, with the Western spelling of 'Brazil'. When I try to spell it as 'Brasil', I am told that I have the spelling wrong (indeed the red dots on the computer are winking at me again as I do it). But surely it is reasonable to allow the people of Brasil/Brazil to decide how to spell the name of their own country? It seems to me the most basic politeness. Some people would call this political correctness, of course, but I would agree with Robert Care at Arup (with its generous and thoughtful founder): '*To my mind, people who cry out that something is PC are just looking for an excuse for bad behaviour.*'

If you get the words right, I think the mind follows. Conversely, if you don't, the mind stays stuck.

Matt Hyde was with the National Union of Students in the UK and is now with the Scouts, so he has represented young people for a long time now. His view on language is very clear: '*Words matter, and they matter a lot. People just have to learn to be a bit more polite. Don't use words that upset other people, or put them down. A really easy example: don't refer to young leaders as "kids". It's rude, and it makes you look ignorant. If you call young leaders "kids", it's no surprise when you find yourself treating them like kids, and then they switch off. Trust has gone out of the window, and it's unlikely to return.*' Matt admits that it can be exhausting (and even embarrassing) to challenge people on this, but it's important: '*Those of us who witness this stuff should push back and tell people to get some CQ, and fast, because if you let things go unchallenged, the mindset establishes itself and festers, and the generations start to clash.*'

Read again what Matt said about the word 'kids'. I think you can replace it with lots of other words, in different contexts. Some might be worse than others, but they all affect trust between the speaker and the people listening. Words need to Flex. As Kingsley Wheaton at British American Tobacco says, '*With words, you have to engage with others on a one-way basis: their way.*'

A final thought on language. If your first language is English, maybe now is the time to learn another one.

Physical issues

In the first part of the book, I talked about getting behaviours right as a first step to developing CQ. I'm coming back to physical issues as an aspect of calibrating Flex, because I know that lots of people genuinely struggle with them. Deciding how you eat, or when to bow; what you can show (legs? head? feet?) and what you can't; how to greet, and how to part. They all matter enormously, and they can all create impressions that well-meant words often can't correct.

To me, all these issues are deeply in Flex: I am perfectly happy to adapt to the situation I am in and the people I am with. This means that I am doubly required to Flex, because for others they are sometimes in deep Core. For me, there are very few physical issues which belong in my Core.

However I did find one recently. I was sitting in Trafalgar Square waiting for a friend, and someone walked by, clearing his throat very loudly. He then spat out the result. He didn't hit me, he just spat it out on the street. Noisily. It's not the first time someone has spat in front of me, and I recoiled as I always do. But, this time, I was thinking hard about Core and Flex. However hard I tried, I don't think I could ever move my disgust at this habit from my Core to my Flex. However many times I tell myself that people in other cultures do things differently. However much I have tried to convince myself that spitting might be part of someone else's Core, and that I should learn to understand it. The truth is, I don't think it could possibly be in anyone's Core. It could well be in their Flex and they refuse to Flex on it, but in Trafalgar Square, I think they probably should. Someone should tell him. I tried, but he just looked at me blankly and walked on. Am I culturally stuck? Or culturally ignorant? Or culturally intolerant? Or should he learn to Flex? And if we were both on a street in another country, am I the one who should learn to Flex?

Physical issues are tough, and all the tougher if you are a woman. The parameters for men are wider; for women they are very narrow. There are some pretty set views on what women should wear and do, and there are no easy answers.

Recently, I went to a very high-profile meeting in India, at which the strong and powerful of India were gathered. I was one of three women there from the UK. Both of the others wore saris. One wore it as if she always had. The other as if she never had – she was constantly tucking her scarf out of the way and wriggling her waist in obvious discomfort. I was in trousers and a jacket. Were they trying to be what they were not, ignoring their Core? Or were they right to treat clothes as Flex which needs to adapt?

The only real answer is to ask. Gavin Dyer in South Africa does: '*Handshakes fascinate me. There are masses of them in Africa. I think*

Ghanaians have the most beautiful one. I only discovered because I asked about it, and I asked them to teach me. I had to do it three times before I got it right. It involves the index and middle finger in a way that when you pull away, there is a clicking sound. Other African shakes have some neat hand and thumb movements, but this is the best. It's not like the South African one, which is a competition to see who can crush more bones. There, you have to approach the other person with your fingers splayed out ready, so that you can be ready to protect them from cracking.'

So keep asking; and listen to the answers. Keep Flexing. The lack of simple answers is frustrating, and you will have to make some fine calls. Just make them openly and honestly. As my father always said about all leadership, *'It's about doing something. If it proves to be the right thing, do more of it, and if it's not the right thing, then apologise and do something else.'*

With all his experience of doing business in different countries, Etienne de Villiers has it right: *'As I have travelled, I have got more tactile, not less. But this is not right for all cultures. You need to check it out.'*

And keep checking.

Humour matters

Everyone has an opinion on humour and CQ. For some, it's an ice-breaker when you're operating in different cultures. For others, it's the quickest way to kill CQ. As I have talked to people around the world about CQ, I have picked up a wide range of views on humour. It certainly polarises opinions, which maybe just goes to show how careful you need to be.

Here's a quick sample of what people told me:

Etienne de Villiers is very clear on it: *'Humour is still the greatest ice-breaker.'*

But diplomat Graham Boyce takes the opposite view. His firm advice to young diplomatic staff is to leave humour at home: *'Don't do jokes. They don't translate.'*

Mike Brearley highlights the value of using humour to express British-ness at its very best: *'The opening ceremony of the London Olympics was that: zany and self-deprecating at the same time.'*

Firoz Patel sees it from two points of view, British and Indian, and he disagrees: '*The British sense of humour is the last bastion of British superiority. We British think that our humour is better than anyone else's.*'

It can clearly cause problems when senses of humour don't match, or jokes aren't (or can't be) shared.

Artistic Director Jude Kelly: '*I have seen people almost bullying others into accepting their sense of humour.*'

Di Schneider in South Africa: '*White people have jokes with sexual innuendo which many black South Africans don't find funny.*' As HR Director, Di has also had to deal with the damage: '*Most of the disciplinary issues which arise within the firm are the result of jokes falling on deaf ears, followed by that killer line "you people are too serious and sensitive".*'

Graham Boyce again: '*You could make an Arab joke to an Arab audience, but not to a British one. And slapstick or visual humour works just about everywhere – Mr Bean is hugely popular – in a way that verbal humour doesn't.*'

Jude Kelly agrees: '*You have to accept that there are different senses of humour and they are culturally specific.*'

Of course, the stakes get raised when the humour has a specific target; when teasing tips into satire; when the laughter hurts someone.

Everyone seems to agree with Reuel Khoza: '*I like laughing, but not at people. I think I have a love-hate relationship with satire. You can make people laugh without leaving the target of your joke hurt, whether they admit it or not.*'

Etienne De Villiers identifies the distinction: '*Teasing is good, ridiculing is not. You can tease people about the weather, or the surroundings, or even sometimes the food, but not about national or individual characteristics. Such teasing is reserved for close friends only. I have seen the British sense of humour, with caustic put-downs, produce a zero-sum game too often, and I can hear the guilty party muttering to themselves, "the foreigner hasn't got a sense of humour".*'

Firoz Patel says that there is an exception to this rule in India: '*Politicians, of course. Everyone in India does politics, we almost all know what is going on and we can't take them seriously. The Indian sport it to caricature them.*'

It's not confined to India. Caricaturing politicians is a global sport. But, in the context of CQ, there's an interesting difference between satirising your own politicians and ridiculing other people's. It's a fine line that comedians from ethnic and religious minorities have been treading for years, too.

Graham Boyce's advice about the culturally specific nature of humour rang in my ears recently. Many British people regard their particular sense of humour as being Core to them, and one of the trickier elements of the British sense of humour is teasing. We're happy to tease ourselves while we're doing it, but we certainly like to tease others. This often gets me in a real mess. A while ago, I jumped on a plane late one afternoon to go to Germany to make a speech. I had worked flat out all day, and I worked even more on the flight. I hardly even noticed the plane landing. Then I dashed for a taxi and made it to the venue just a little bit late. I went straight on to the platform and never took the time to take in that this was not a British audience. When the question-and-answer session started, I teased the audience – a lot. It went down like a lead balloon. I could see them almost physically taking a step back, folding their arms against me, the people at the back even leaning against the back wall with their arms firmly crossed and their chins up in the air. Everything I had said in my talk evaporated from the room. I got it wrong from the minute I walked in. To make it worse, I realised that I had not eaten all day. So on the way in, I grabbed a banana. When the call came to go on the platform, I handed it to the first obvious person. Apparently, he is still smarting from this totally unintended lack of respect.

Peter Kulloi in Hungary says humour is always high-risk: *'When I was 29, I started a consultancy company. I got a call one day from the PA of a very big player in Austria, who wanted to talk about buying two companies in Hungary. I was to go to lunch to meet him. It was a huge table, many waiters, silver everywhere, everyone speaking German. He said something to the gathering. And I chose to turn it into a pun, a funny pun. His spoon stopped on the way to his mouth and there was at least 20 seconds of silence. It was a long, long time, during which time I lost two kilos. Then he laughed, and I thought, I have risked the great break of my career for a pun. Since then, I have been very careful with my sense of humour. It worked that day – just – but it could just as easily have gone the other way and ruined a very important opportunity. I was not respectful enough. I was a nobody.'*

The most comprehensive analysis of the strengths and weaknesses of using humour came from Alan Rosling, a businessman who grew up in Britain and has been working in India for many years: *'You need things to help you connect across cultures, to lubricate things. With some cultures, sharing food or alcohol helps. Although you can make incredible mistakes. As a young man, I invited a Hindu friend to supper and arranged a beef fondue. The table was stacked high with large bits of raw beef. I look back on that night with horror. Crucially, she forgave me, because we laughed – at me. Speaking many languages helps a lot if you want to build CQ. Being patently honest helps too, and so does humour, but I do have some advice on humour:*

1. *Be careful: jokes don't travel.*

2. *You have to laugh with people, and not at them.*

3. *Find something that you can both laugh about together. It is very helpful for me that the British are so hopeless at cricket; it means that I can always get a laugh if I laugh at British cricket.*

4. *Teasing is good – but not until you know people well.*

5. *Best of all: laugh at yourself.*

Yes, you get it wrong all the time, but the most common mistake with humour is to go too fast. Gauge the person a bit first – even if it is only quickly.

I screwed up my visa application when I was going to Vietnam. I put the wrong date on it. When I arrived, I joked with the immigration officer that I was so keen on Vietnam, I had come early. She sorted it all out for me there and then as we laughed together: again, at me.

I discussed all this with Mark Linder, who has managed communications for a wide variety of global brands during his time at WPP, and now Bell Pottinger. He summarised humour like this: *'There are jokes: they don't translate. Then there is humour: this bonds. Then there is laughter: and this helps you get over mistakes.'*

My conclusion? There's no simple answer. But I do know that humour carries a large sign that reads 'Proceed with extreme caution'.

Local knowledge

When you're calibrating Flex, you can't fly blind. You need to know what you are Flexing *to*. So you need genuine local knowledge.

There are two relatively simple ways to get it. The first is to ask local people and listen (fiercely) to their answers. The second is to Flex the Flex. When you do this, people are generous; they tell you how the world looks through their eyes. If you listen and Flex (as well as sticking to your Core), then slowly you build up local knowledge, and with it, CQ.

Common Purpose is starting to do more work in China. So, recently, I asked a leader in China to tell me about the country. It wouldn't be fair to name him, so I won't, but I did listen fiercely to what he said. He told me what he thinks lies at the heart of why Chinese and Western leaders simply do not understand each other: '*I have come to understand that we approach problems very differently in China, and in a way that makes other people very uncomfortable. We mix things up. My German colleague will want to go from A to B to C. I will give a little on C, want you to give on A and we can talk about B. Chinese people are disciplined – but we don't like precision. Our attachment to discipline is based on how we see power: the power of the government over the citizen, the parent over the child, the boss over the employee. We obey commandments, but we are not precise. We also like to look at the whole picture and weave our way around it.*

Let me give you an example. If I go to the Chinese doctor about a stomach ache, he will put his hand to my wrist and that's where he will diagnose me. Then he will do acupuncture on my leg, and then my stomach ache will go away. If I explain this to a Western doctor, they think I am crazy. They say, this isn't medicine, it's witchcraft, magic. How could there possibly be a relationship between the leg, the wrist and the stomach? And I look at him in wonder as he ends up suggesting putting a probe into my stomach for no good reason. For me and the Chinese doctor, the body is a whole and the stomach is only one part of it. In this company, the Western doctors ask the Chinese to explain and, when they do, they all end up confused.'

As we spoke, I was dealing with a struggle between a Chinese and a Western colleague. They both say that the other is being illogical. The Chinese guy is jumping from here to there, and refuses to explain his thinking to the Westerner, who has accused him of being irrational.

The Western guy has lost all patience and refuses to accept any jumping in logic. They both think the other one is crazy, and maybe neither is. Maybe there are sequences in the jump which the Westerner has to consider and the Chinese manager has to take the time to analyse.

So I go on asking my Chinese contact and listen to him. He tells me the story of his bosses: '*First I had a Chinese manager, then I had an Indian one. He was a surprise and a big change. He talked to me, sought out my ideas, encouraged all of us in our team. I was used to having bosses who behaved as my parents: they told me what to do, by when and how to do it, and I was to do it fast. My Indian boss was full of ideas and was far less disciplined, but we did have some very good ideas. We were slower: things get done much faster under a Chinese boss, but you tend to be repeating the same things. I worked well with the Indian boss because I am Chinese and so I am disciplined, so we complemented each other.*

Then I had an Australian boss, who operated out of Singapore. I don't know if he is typical of Australians, but he was very noisy. He was a big guy, he gave you masses of freedom, he was great at talking and having ideas. But he was arrogant, and he admitted it himself and laughed about it. He said he was from an island and that's how island people are. His confidence was huge, completely different from my Indian boss. I suppose he and I are from developing countries so we are more cautious. My Australian boss provided real structure and we had more colourful and more adventurous discussions. He also opened my eyes to the rest of the world. But I would only take him to meet English-speaking leaders in China who are Westernised, and even they tended to just watch him. They would remain quiet and listen to the big Western guy, talking with great gestures. He never lost us a deal because we never had difficult deals to do, so we could remain superficial. But if we had had difficult times and needed to negotiate something tricky, I think there would have been a problem. He just didn't show enough respect. He was casual and democratic, and Chinese people are very serious. He didn't give people enough "face". If you do that, everything becomes negotiable. But once you have lost face, you can't get it back. He would have had to dress more formally, listen more sensitively, use words more carefully. He would have had to stop coming on so strong. His strength came across as arrogance.'

Gavin Dyer in Johannesburg gave me a great example of the frustration that can result when international deadlines meet local ways of doing things: '*I asked one of my direct reports in Africa for some figures. There were some difficult decisions to be made, we were under real pressure to make them and I needed some facts and figures. Instead of giving me the information I asked for, he sent me an email about a crocodile and a fish. I vividly recall my response when I got it: "What the hell is this idiot up to?" I am not certain what I might have done next. The pressure to pin down what we were going to do on the issue was intense, and I thank my lucky stars that he said this, via email, from a long distance. If we had been in the same room, face to face, I think I might have lost his respect for life. But then my secretary told me to hold on and, instead of just getting angry, work out what he was trying to say.*

The truth was that he was telling me that I was going down the wrong route in my thinking. What he was saying – using an allegory – was to hold off because there was another way to look at the deal and with a better solution. It was a pretty scary experience and, without doubt, a watershed moment for me. One of those moments you recall forever, when real learning took place. I moved on from it – and then came back to it a few weeks later when I was on the CSCLeaders programme, with a lot of other leaders from Africa. I was brought up in the Western way of thinking and the Western way of leading. I deal in facts, and I communicate through facts. If you are brought up in the African tradition, you deal in stories, and you communicate your message through stories. The two cultures don't have to clash: they can be very effective together, but only if I get better at seeing the message in the story – and my colleague gets better at judging what I needed in stressful situations.'

So you listen for good local knowledge, and then you just have to keep Flexing the Flex, when the temptation is always there not to.

Konstantin Mettenheimer in Frankfurt picks up the theme of handling meetings: '*As a German, you arrive on time for a meeting – and this means five minutes before it is due to start. In other cultures, it means five minutes after the time it is due to start. Both are categorised as being "on time" in different cultures. The danger is that you sit there, as a German, getting angry because the others seem rude in your eyes. They are simply late, and this is rude. Especially when you have arrived on time. So you have to learn to check yourself. You don't have to like it, but you do have to resist the instinct or temptation to be offended.*' And then he adds, '*We Germans have to learn to live with ambiguity too. And that is even harder than time-keeping.*'

Eric Thomas describes learning to Flex to Japanese meetings: '*Somehow, you have to understand that a meeting in the West is where you air ideas, put issues on the table, discuss them, resolve the conflicts and then, crucially, you make decisions and decide the outcomes. In Japan, a meeting is only about exchanging information: it goes no further. So, if a Western executive flies across the world to Japan for a meeting and then leaves thinking that a decision has been made, they are kidding themselves. More likely, they will discover later that no decision has been made and they'll think that something is wrong.'*

Vandana Saxena Poria is a young entrepreneur in India (she is CEO of educational publisher Get Through Guides). She describes the need to be able to Flex constantly in her professional life: *'You just do have to learn to adapt. I am already a woman, which clients find hard to deal with, because very few people in business in India are seen as "women": they are daughters-in-law, mothers or wives. (India is completely dominated by men. Don't be fooled by the tiny number of exceptions to this.) How I treat the CEO of a global Indian business and the CEO of a family-owned Indian business bear no resemblance to each other. With the first, I will use first names; with the second, I will say "sir". With the first, I will reveal that I am a professional woman with two children, who travels for work; with the second, such words would never be uttered (they would assume that my children were abandoned). The former would not be interested in who my Chairman was; the latter would want to know (and know that it is my husband – this seems to give legitimacy in their minds, that business could be discussed with me). I will adapt not just my words but my speed of talking, the subjects I use to establish a rapport and, crucially, how I show deference.'*

And it is not just in business that you have to be able to Flex. I have a friend who worked as a hospital doctor for many years: *'That's when I really learnt to Flex. Try running a surgical ward when everything goes wrong and it's clear that your junior doctors have made mistakes. So you meet with them, and a young African doctor sits there, smiling broadly at you, as if all the world was wonderful and easy, when the reality is desperate. It took me a considerable time to recognise that many Africans smile when they are stressed. It is not some smug denial of what has just happened: it's stress, excessive stress. I learnt the hard way to resist the temptation to reach conclusions long before I started to ask questions.'*

As I said earlier in the book, you can't spend your whole life seeing the world through other people's eyes, but you can get a great deal better at it than you are now. Flexing may even become second nature. As Riz Ahmed says, *'Now that I am down to my Core, the rest is wonderful, fluid Flex.'*

Understand pride, or 'face'

While I have been writing this book and meeting the people who have played their part in it, there have been moments when I have very clearly seen something that I had not seen before, and have almost certainly been getting wrong.

One such moment had been brewing ever since I first met Mike Brearley, and he described captaining a team with star players in it. He said, '*It takes a while to realise, but they need just as much recognition as the rest, and sometimes a great deal more.*' Sometimes when a batsman was bowled out, you could tease him as he walked back into the dressing room: '*My granny could have kept that out.*' And the batsman would smile wryly and chuckle, and that would have taken the heat out of the moment. But sometimes when the batsman came off, you had to say something like, '*You have just been bowled out by the best ball ever bowled in the entire history of the game of cricket.*' Because, if you didn't say this – however great a cricketer he was – the man's pride would be crushed, and if you threw him the joke about your granny, you would have made it a great deal worse.

Leaders who want CQ need to understand pride in people, and the source of that pride, and it varies across cultures greatly.

Months later, Konstantin Mettenheimer made the same point to me: '*Be careful to find out what people are proud of – and be very, very careful not to rubbish it. You should be watching out for it the moment you meet. Red lights should flash when you spot it: glaring warning lights in your head. And it doesn't matter whether you think they should be proud of it or not. Because they are – and that's enough. It's tender territory, rational or not.*'

I think this has been a blind spot for me for some time. It's why I regularly misjudge situations, and it's all because of a piece of my Core that is rooted in a story that's also deep in my Core.

We're going back to grannies. If my grandmother said this to me once when I was a child, she said it to me a hundred times. She'd say it with a sad, critical eye and a slow shake of the head which went deep into her shoulders: '*My girl, pride comes before a fall.*' To me, pride has always been something to be ashamed of. Revealing pride shows that you think too much of yourself. It was knocked into me that pride was what made you blind to reality, and caused you to miscalculate and make bad decisions.

So pride has always been bad, bad, bad for me. Not just the simple word, but all the subtle variations of it. I have certainly always believed that your pride should never ever get in the way of Flexing in situations with other people. It was drummed into me so deep that I didn't really know it was there: it had so fundamentally become part of my story. A combination of Mike and Konstantin blew it out, because I was wrong and they are right, especially in many cultures around the world.

Looking back, I recall a colleague saying to me once, '*I can lose my argument, my money and my friends, but at least I have my pride.*' I just stared back in amazement. This was someone I valued enormously, yet here he was, making an important decision based openly on his pride, because he simply refused to apologise for something he had said. Unashamedly, he was letting pride get in his way and not doing the right thing because of it. From beyond the grave, my grandmother was doing her slow head-shake at me. To me, pride is a concept associated with Flex: you shouldn't let it get in the way. But to my colleague, it was Core: and so Core that he would rather be bankrupt and friendless than apologise. For him, to 'bend down' (as he saw it) was simply inconceivable. This was foreign territory for me and, looking back, I didn't even know it. How could I have dealt with it better? By recognising that this was about his pride (the 'P word') and not pushing back in the way I did, which was to say to myself 'this is all about pride, and that is ridiculous, so I should push harder'.

Just the day before meeting Konstantin Mettenheimer, I had met Peter Kulloi in Budapest. He summed it up: '*It's always ego that gets in the way; that's what most fights are about. Can I be richer, smarter, more powerful, more in the know, more connected? Ego is the problem.*' I had agreed with him, and came away thinking how ridiculous it was. But now I was starting to think that perhaps Peter was trying to tell me that I had to recognise it and deal with it, and not just dismiss it as irrelevant and misguided.

Martin Kalungu-Banda from Zambia gave me a lovely example of a much better way of managing someone else's pride so that no one loses face: '*The women of Africa have learned to get their own way while never undermining their man's pride. My mother learned how to do this with my father. She had never been to school, yet my father was a headmaster. He was the head of the house and he tended to make pronouncements such as "from today onwards, this will not happen". I would then watch my mother honour his position beautifully, and eventually move on from it and completely reverse it, to the extent that when she had finished talking and turned to him for affirmation, he would nod, gladly consenting to the 360-degree reversal which had just taken place.*

Here's an example. In our household, you had one new pair of shoes each year. If something went wrong with them – if they got lost or broken – you went without shoes for the rest of the year, or borrowed ill-fitting cast-offs. I played football and destroyed a pair. My father – in front of my brothers, sisters and cousins – bellowed that even if I was the son of a head teacher, I would go barefoot for months. My mother agreed gently with everything he said, and she told me how terrible it was not to honour my father. And then, slowly, her tirade slipped to saying that I would show that I honoured my father most if I could show that I would not lose the next pair of shoes. Slowly, I was getting my new pair of shoes, and my father was nodding gladly. As long as my mother gave my father the honour he was entitled to, all the rest of the space was left for her to dance on. A lot of pride is the determination not to apologise. Unlike my mother, I sometimes get in the way of this process: by demanding closure in the form of an apology, when it would be better to stand back and watch the person correct things without making them lose face.'

So pride is not necessarily arrogance. Nor is it an irrelevance: quite the opposite. For many people, in many cultures, it is crucial, and it's Core. They won't Flex it, because they can't. So you need to realise it and understand it, rather than dismissing it.

If you get this judgement right, you don't offend people. Even better, you build trust with them. Etienne de Villiers put it beautifully: '*On the whole, it is a good idea that people feel good about themselves through their interaction with you. So go slower. Don't challenge a person until you have taken the time to understand them first.*'

Good advice; good Flex, and very good for CQ.

Exercise: Reassess your Core and Flex

Earlier in the book, as we introduced the concepts of Core and Flex, I invited you to get a piece of paper and write yours down. Now it might be interesting to get the piece of paper and look at again. Is there anything you would add or change? Is there anything you would move? Has the line between Core and Flex shifted? As you look forward, is there anything that might move in the future? If so, why?

For me, this is all part of the airing process. You don't have to do it every day. But, every now and then, as you gather experiences and develop CQ, I think it's useful.

Part Six

Dealing with the opposite of CQ

In the first part of this book, we established two opposites of CQ: cultural intolerance (which certainly exists and is deeply unpleasant) and cultural ignorance (which is lazier and generally more blinkered). Both are a problem, and dealing with each of them requires very different action.

Cultural intolerance

I don't propose to make the argument against cultural intolerance here, for the simple reason that if you have decided to read this book (and have got this far), it is likely that the case against does not need to be made to you. This is about as much attention as I want to give it here; other than to reinforce a couple of points I made earlier.

First, you need to stand up to cultural intolerance when you come across it. Whether it takes 30 seconds or three months, and however embarrassing or difficult it might be to do it. I believe that many leaders in the generation younger than mine recognise this, even if their bosses or parents shy away from it, preferring politeness to confrontation. I believe that my generation has confused CQ with politeness and will maintain the latter at almost any cost.

And, second, you need to recognise the importance of finding the bits of cultural intolerance in yourself, because they are sure to be there, whoever you are. This is true even if you have been the victim of cultural intolerance yourself. Michael Hastings at KPMG says you have to be very careful not to forget this: *'As a member of a minority, I think you have to recognise that you, too, have blinkers. I think that you have to see that all individual freedom is a balancing act with the freedom of others. Suffering as a minority does not mean that your individual freedom should now outweigh this reality. And, if you let it, you become part of the new problem.'*

Some of your own cultural intolerance can be aired and moved on. And some – in the words of my friend who admitted that he would never marry someone from a different caste – is simply 'etched in'. You know you won't be able to move it, let alone remove it. But, if you are honest and brave, you can at least see it for what it is. You can recognise that it is your problem and no one else's, and therefore not impose it on others. Assuming that you cannot eliminate it even if you try, I think the only option you have then is to counterbalance it.

Eric Thomas explained it better than I can: *'Like many people from my own generation, I can say, for example, that if I meet someone who is gay, it makes not an iota of difference to me. It does not register in my thinking at any level. But, if you told me that the person came from certain countries, then questions would jump into my mind, and lots of them. The important thing at this point is consciously and deliberately and very clearly and firmly to talk to yourself and tell yourself to shut up.'*

And you need to keep talking to yourself. Because, pretty much wherever you are, there will be people around you who are very firmly doing the opposite. Alan Rosling again: *'Having been brought up in the West, I have been programmed not to comment on people's difference: to cut (or at least try to cut) people's backgrounds out of my assessment of them. Being in India for so many years has challenged this. When an Indian leader meets another Indian leader, they are analysing from the first moment they speak where they are from, what social background, what wealth. They put each other in boxes very fast. Of course, we do it too, but Indians are the experts, the masters at this. They pin people down in minutes, and there is a real danger that you will catch this habit if you are not very careful.'*

Cultural ignorance

Because cultural ignorance is less aggressive, less premeditated and less deliberate, I do think it's worth spending more time here on how to avoid it, and I would like to offer three pieces of advice.

Beware of generalisation

Be careful of the human tendency to generalise, to string together a series of apparently connecting facts to produce unreliable but apparently equally logical conclusions. For example: 'I met a man from Commonville who drank too much; so I conclude that all people from Commonville are drunks.' This results in the blindness of cultural ignorance. When a leader turns specific experiences into a general theory, and then claims that it is based on experience, or simply muddles lots of pieces of information and aggregates them into an overall view.

It is something that we all do, all the time. Using the word 'everyone' with a capital E. Saying things like 'The problem with you lot is . . .'. Or 'You're all the same . . .' (that's always guaranteed to wind people up, in my experience). But it can be subtler too. Take the phrase 'Let me explain this to you . . .'. I hear this across all sectors, and I get it myself when someone from the private sector thinks that because I work in an NGO, I am stupid, dodgy, vague, flakey, muddled or all of them at once. It used to outrage me. Now it tires me. (Although I must admit that sometimes it empowers me: it can be very useful to be underestimated.)

Bella Matambanadzo in Zimbabwe describes a more debilitating effect of the tendency to generalise: '*There is a presumption of male leadership which makes women leading much harder. If a man walks into the room it is presumed, in most of the world, that he will lead. I worked for a female manager once. She was called Patricia, which was usually shortened to Pat. She was considered to be a man by most. When people realised that she was a woman, their conscious or unconscious response was to blank her. They would un-negotiate deals with her, even around her pay. We called it the "urinal syndrome". Decisions were made in breaks, in the urinals, and then officiated when the meeting regathered. For a woman, it is very hard to get in on a culture that's designed to keep you out. You didn't have a seat at the table when your dowry was decided or when you daughters' dowries were decided, so why would you be allowed in a boardroom?*'

What she is describing doesn't apply only between men and women. It happens with young and old; public sector and private; and from country to country. Although people like to defend it on the grounds of logic, generalisation is not logical on many fronts.

For a start, the basis for generalisation is constantly shifting. Gary Phillips is the headmaster of the Lilian Baylis Technology School in South London, where more than 40 languages are spoken. He puts it very well: *'In the school, like attracts like: with like defined as "what is important to me". At different times, different things frame what "like" is based on. In the past, it was race. Now, in the school, it is more aspiration and class.'*

My South African colleague Elsbeth Dixon gives another example of ignorance changing over generations: *'In South Africa, our parents' ignorance was that black people were different from white. Our generation's ignorance is probably that we are different from other Africans.'*

Generalisations are often made on inaccurate data, too. As Khadija Rhoda, at university in Johannesburg, says, *'The expression "my kind" is too often presumed to be based on race or culture. People assume that because I wear a headscarf, that's what "my kind" must be based on. But they are wrong. The people I choose to spend time with share my interests: that's what forms "my kind" for me. My group of friends are of different faiths and races. We share education, and ideas about women.'*

Pauline Lafferty at Weir in Glasgow gave me another example: *'Too often, you are looking at the wrong diversity. You think about countries and forget that some urban groups are increasingly the same the world over. Certainly, some local mining communities are pretty much the same wherever you go.'*

You can't even generalise about one family. I have five children, and one is more reflective than the others. It's not a stage or a phase, she just is, and reflective people come in all shapes and sizes the world over.

Of course, generalisation can also produce entirely ridiculous outcomes. As Etienne de Villiers says, *'In the US, people respond to my South African accent – which they think is so sophisticated, even erudite – by allocating me an extra 30 points on my IQ.'*

Develop judgement; avoid pre-judgement

The sort of thinking that tends towards generalisation also generates pre-judgement, which is often based on inadequate or unconnected facts that may, in any case, be out of date. It forms the basis, however, for all kinds of 'fact-based' opinions, judgements and decisions.

I went straight to my risk management friend on this, because I thought he must be dealing with the issue on a daily basis. And he is: *'The first thing I'd say is that judgement and pre-judgement are not equals. Pre-judgement is just a bad working of judgement: there is nothing sound about it. You avoid it primarily by using analytics. You look at the data with a clear, clean head. Some people avoid this, in case the data does not confirm their views, and some claim that data can prove anything. Well, the wrong data can, but you have to be honest and look at the right data – and at all the data, not just a part. You have to get as many facts as possible, even if you don't like them. In fact, especially if you don't like them. I always say that people are entitled to their own opinions, but not to their own facts. You must know the distinction – and be honest about it. As you do this, it's worth remembering two things. First, that facts get out of date very quickly nowadays. There is so much information around and much of it becomes obsolete quickly: especially on the Internet. And, secondly, you must remember that Google filters the information it gives to you, depending on what it is programmed to think that you think. This is a bit of a mouthful, but here's a way to test it. Ask someone with very different search habits from you to Google the same thing you are Googling. Different articles will come up. So, even what we see as facts are actually judgements on which facts someone has decided they think you want to hear.'*

Not that all pre-judgements are lazy or manipulated. Pre-judgement can spring from passion or commitment too. Over the years, I have (perhaps too often) become passionate about making something happen and passionate about how important it is. You will need this passion if you are to achieve the apparently impossible, because it often is impossible. I was asked recently about how, as a leader, you decide where to be on a 'wave of change'. If you are too far back, you can miss the wave. If you are too far ahead, you can get crushed. I thought for a while and admitted that most of the time, I am not sure that I am on 'the wave' at all. I'm in the water, paddling away, trying to get myself and the project to the beach in one piece.

To bring about change, you often have to fight the forces of lethargy, so you need passion to sustain you, to keep you going, to make your case again and yet again, to draw people in and to inspire them (and often to keep others out and prevent them from stopping things). This passion is crucial, but it can also produce your own form of pre-judgement. You become so passionate about your argument that you see only the data that reinforces it and the people who agree with you become the only people you hear. Amali de Alwis, in Geneva, said the same: '*You have to allow for people not to fit the pattern you see, to buck the trend. Even assuming that you have spotted the trend accurately.*'

A friend introduced me to the word 'anecdata'. It refers to information that is based only on anecdotes, which we then turn into data and allow to form our opinions, often based on our conviction that what we do is likely to be the best, or at least the starting point, and possibly the benchmark of success as well. Former British ambassador Graham Boyce says we all have our convictions of how things should be done, and we simply cannot compute that other people have ways that might work at all, never mind work better: '*For a state visit, we would do six to nine months of detailed preparation. Then President Mubarak came in to the office one day and said he wanted to do a state visit at lunchtime. It was the first such visit to be made in 18 years, and it went off just as well. Why is our approach better?*'

So my banking friend's analytical approach feels right, at least as a starting point. Then, he says, '*You need a mindset that is driven by (1) knowing that all decisions must be informed by facts and data; (2) having the self-awareness that we have inbuilt biases; (3) being teachable and open to learning; (4) being open to challenge and having your judgements challenged.*'

Form your own opinions

Just as I went to my banking friend on the subject of facts, I went to Jon Williams at ABC in New York on opinions. He says that today, we all have to get better at forming our own opinions: '*You need to be informed by others but have the strength to have your own views and then do what you believe is right. Of course, be informed by the media, but don't be slavish to it, and take care not to just hear the loudest voices. Synthesise what you hear from many sources and don't abdicate the responsibility to form your own view.*' Then he gave me the punchline I have written above my desk: '*People need to form opinions, not catch them.*'

Here's a small but telling example from my brother, who keeps horses. It's about a man I have never met, but whom I admire enormously. One of the events in the Summer Olympics is the modern pentathlon, a mixture of pistol shooting, fencing, swimming, cross-country running and show jumping. For the last event, competitors are given a horse they have never ridden and just 20 minutes to ride it for the first time. You can also speak briefly to the horse's groom. Then you have to do a round of about 12 very high jumps, with penalties if you hit a fence or the horse refuses. The organisers select 40 suitable horses and allocate them to riders randomly. In 2012, they chose my brother's horse Trini (short for Trinidad). She was an unusual selection because she was significantly smaller than all the other horses – and ugly too (she is a strawberry roam, speckled red, brown and white). The other horses were huge and sleek, and looked the part.

A Hungarian rider got Trini. He was trailing far behind from the previous events, and his heart must have sunk when he saw her. Then he met her groom: a short young woman who cannot have looked the part to him either. She told him not to be put off, but that Trini had a habit of letting out a huge fart as she went over every jump. His heart must have sunk to his riding boots. She also gave him a piece of advice: *'Don't ride Trini. Just sit on her, hold on and she will do it. If you tell her what to do, she will stumble.'* He made an instant judgement to trust a far from elegant and embarrassingly noisy horse who was tiny for the job, and to trust a groom who did not fit the image, and follow her advice. It must have seemed counter-intuitive, since they were big jumps and reading the course, tracing the best route and calculating the numbers of steps between each jump is what show jumping is all about. But he took the advice, climbed into the saddle and let Trini get on with it. They did a clear round (one of very few on the day), and he finished the overall pentathlon with a bronze medal.

Even in a nanosecond, his decision proved right. So work out who to trust – and then form your own opinions, because 'received wisdom' (and all the assumptions it brings with it) can catch you out.

Put yourself on the receiving end

As you struggle with your own cultural ignorance, I think you also have to understand what it's like to be on the receiving end of it, particularly if you have little experience of it yourself. I discussed this with a variety of leaders who have experienced both cultural ignorance and cultural intolerance and I asked them to tell me how it made them feel.

Angry

My young British–Turkish doctor friend told me, '*I have never really experienced racism which has upset me, but I get called a "Paki" a lot – and I just get furious, even though I know it's their problem, not mine. The ignorant fools.*'

South African student Khadija says she is worried that it puts her into a permanent state of fighting: '*My father brought me up to believe that we are all the same; to have a deep sense of justice which was rooted in his religion. I am Cape Malay, my friends are not, and they were always welcomed at home. So, when I came to get married, it was a huge shock for me that it all became so very different, because he is black, but I was shocked. This was not what my father had taught me – and it showed that they didn't know me at all. My mother was not against him, but she was deeply shocked, and the rest of the family were in uproar. They thought that I had chosen him as some sort of act of desperation: why else would I choose a man who did not fit my status? From many, the cry was "But how will we explain him to our friends?". It was an awful time. The result is that I am always up for a fight. It has become almost my default position, and I am starting to worry about myself. I am starting to see fights even where they don't actually exist. We went to a wedding last week, an Indian wedding. We went together expecting antagonism, because they had been the most aggressive when we had wanted to marry. Their response wrongfooted us completely: they were lovely. It has made me think that we need to expose ourselves to more pleasant experiences, otherwise we will see fights everywhere where they might not actually exist.*'

Cynical

Police officer Ellie Bird describes a different reaction: '*You become very cynical, because you can see it happening. I am used to prejudice because I'm a woman, so I'm attuned to it. But, for a change, it was about my religion. At interview, they were desperate to find out if I was Catholic or Protestant. So they asked me where I went to school, and what teams I supported. They dug around to get me to reveal the names of my parents and friends, and they asked me how many siblings I have (the assumption being that if I come from a big family, I must be Catholic). They even tried to find out what my favourite colour was by asking about my clothes. Did I like to wear orange or green? Red or blue? These things are very revealing in Glasgow.'*

Tired

Michael Hastings at KPMG described to me the tiredness even the powerful and successful can feel in the face of cultural intolerance, or even casual ignorance: *'Each year, I take part in a sponsored walk for Zimbabwe relief. We help people in need, both black and white. I get an enormous amount of flak for the fact that we support both: but the truth is that there are many white people who have lost everything. On the last leg of the most recent walk, the lead walker stopped at a Manor House outside Oxford. As the walkers came in, they heard a voice ringing down the corridor: "I hope none of the money is going to the niggers". No one answered. Why? Because we were tired. We were overwhelmed by the authority with which the man made his assumptions. We didn't want to have to muster up the counterbalancing force required to meet them, and we knew that we would probably look foolish if we did anything other than full blast. But we all left with the usual feeling when you do nothing. In situations like that we all feel full of guilt. We feel stupid and pathetic and gutless, and we know we have not been strong enough. We knew we had let everything and everyone down. Long afterwards, reflecting on all the things that maybe should have been said, had we not been so tired, I realised that it had made the tiredness so much greater, and I sensed too how it must feel to face it every day.'*

Crushed

David Isaac is a partner at law firm Pinsent Masons in London. He is also the former Chair of Stonewall, the largest gay equality organisation in Europe. He tells the story of a friend standing waiting for a lift. The lift was very slow to arrive and the young man standing next to David's friend muttered, "This lift is so gay". He meant the lift was defective and broken. David says: *"It's an expression that young people use increasingly in the UK, and it makes anyone – my friend, and me too – feel crushed and demeaned. Notwithstanding all the legislative progress we have made in the UK to establish legal equality for gay people, it is really depressing to find that the next generation are using the word "gay" in this way. It shows the power of language to reinforce cultural intolerance, and the thoughtless way in which negative images of gay people can be perpetuated. How to respond? By ridiculing them in a clever witty way, probably. Their response – I can predict*

*it – would vary from "It's only a word, don't overreact" to "Are you gay?",
and, from there, things often spiral downwards."*

Old

Last year, I did a talk at a business school. Having found the time and
made my way there, I noticed that as I was speaking, at least half the
group were just working on their laptops. They were not taking notes;
they were simply doing something else while I was talking to them. I was
put off at first. Then flustered. Then pressurised, as I tried to say over-
the-top things to get their attention. And then I just got very angry. The
way I dealt with it made me the rude one, of course. It made me feel
cheap and irrelevant and, for the first time in my life, old. It was a horrible experience, and one that I would not repeat. They learnt nothing
from me. I didn't even get the satisfaction that I had wasted an hour of
their time. They made good use of it, but it was nothing to do with me.

But then I watched my 17-year-old son watching a film on TV, while he
emailed, and checked his Facebook status, and texted, and chatted,
every now and then to me. He somehow took it all in, all at the same
time. My anger at the business school students was real, for me, but
maybe they didn't deserve it. 'My bad'. Well, my need to Flex, anyway.

Disengaged

Remember my colleague Genevieve Barr describing the opposite effect
– when a speaker's arrogance loses the audience: *'At any time, there's a very
thin line you have to tread between appearing arrogant and knowledgeable. But,
in disability, the line becomes razor-sharp, because arrogance is associated with
people thinking that they are superior. The antennae of disabled people are very
acute on this. Given all the stigmas around disability, arrogance is not tolerated
well. As young disabled leaders, we immediately became disengaged.'*

Frustrated

Bella Matambanadzo in Zimbabwe: *'Imagine how it feels, as a woman,
when you get into a taxi in a city you know well. The taxi driver is a dude and
will go his way, certainly not some woman's way, and he won't take your
advice, even when he gets totally lost. You sit in the back, seething with frustration. Well, the same thing happens all the time. Women get into power now,
but they can't shift the policy, because the culture is set by leaders who are all*

men. You get so frustrated at having got through the door, but not being able to influence the agenda.'

Weak

Michael Hastings again: *'You do begin to realise how weak you are. And how, even after a pretty successful career, you can be undermined so quickly. I was in Beijing, sitting on a wall outside a big museum opposite the People's Party headquarters. Two Chinese people in their early twenties came over to me and said "Nigger, nigger . . ." to attract my attention. They were speaking in faltering English, and were trying to ask me about the way in to the museum. I just stared at them in amazement. Sure, they didn't speak good English, but this was no excuse for calling me a nigger. I was so utterly furious that I walked away fast and carried my anger with me to the airport. I was sitting there in a tea shop, and I heard another person calling me "nigger". I swung around fast, assuming that the nasty young couple had followed me, but I couldn't see them, so I just left. I felt really bruised and battered and hurt and shocked and depressed by it.*

Three months later, when the feelings had lost their edge, I spoke to a Chinese delegation. They had a young interpreter with them, and I asked her to help me understand it. When I told her the story, she started to laugh. In Mandarin, "Ni-eer" is an interrupting sound: a noise you make when you are stumbling in your speech and trying to form the next words. A bit like "uuuum" or "errrr" in English. I sat down and looked at the wound I had been carrying for three months, at the deep sense of upset and desperation. I should have asked them, there and then. Instead, I absorbed the offence. I suppose that I felt that, in the light of their ignorance or intolerance, the best thing to do was to accept it, when all I had to do was to say something. I am The Lord Hastings, a leader at KPMG, I travel the world to speak to huge audiences and I am so gutted by the apparent use of the word "nigger" by two young Chinese kids that I become speechless, and then wounded for three months. I tell this story to young people now with the message "deal with it". Because, when you do, you might be surprised by the response.'

Mystified

My oldest friend, Margo, is German. She describes an experience at university that has stayed with her: *'If you are German, sometimes things fly out of nowhere. I had a British tutor who went into agonies if the word "war" was used. It's difficult to avoid when you are studying history – but he would get all heated, and glance at me nervously, and then desperately try to change the subject as fast as he could. He made an assumption around my sensitivity on the issue that was ludicrous. It's part of my heritage, my cultural make-up. This sort of thing happens occasionally and, when it does, you say to yourself, "Where did that one come from?"'*

Intimidated

Perhaps more insidious is the feeling that you have to surrender to a confident view, held by a majority from which you are excluded, so you play down your own talents and strength and end up conforming to the very stereotype that is being imposed on you.

Michael Hastings puts it well: *'Somehow, you must not let the intolerant intimidate you with their confident view of the world. However successful you are, if you are not careful, they sort of swallow you up with their assumptions; when you are faced with their very clear view of the world, with you in a certain part of it.'*

Bella agrees: *'You do learn to cope. Some people flirt their way through, but then you are stuck in a role that limits you. In my country, we are taught, almost from birth, to "dim your light", so that you don't overshadow the people who think they are superior to you!'*

It is a challenge to the next generation to be better at all this than mine has been. Not to confuse politeness with cultural intelligence as mine has, and not simply to aspire to be better, but to take the risks and actually be so. To have the conversations; sort their own demons; and respond to cultural ignorance and intolerance (because they both do damage).

I am not even sure that my generation will understand this plea. So the new generation who do will need to do it all in the knowledge that many of their bosses don't understand it, but this should not bother them too much, because their peers will understand it, and they will be running the world soon.

Part Seven

Experiencing experience

We've already discussed the circular nature of CQ. You can only get CQ if people will give it to you; and they will only give it to you if they sense that you have enough CQ to receive it. So CQ is over-whelmingly acquired through experience. Going to places and talking to people where they are. But there's more to it than travel. I think the trick is to make sure that you actually experience the experiences, rather than simply collecting them like stamps on a passport.

For some people this seems to be natural. A friend of mine, Margaret Schmidt, is now, in her words, 'adjusting to being old'. Having spent her life in the majority, she tells me that she is learning to be in a minority (and a pretty marginalised one, since people assume that given her age, she must be slow and slightly dim). Margaret has travelled the world in her career, having left her village in Wales after World War Two to take up a scholarship in the US. It was natural for her: *'Some of us were born with a third eye. We wanted to see more, do more, hear more and experience more than the people around us.'*

Donna Hrinak runs Boeing in Brazil, having been a US diplomat for most of her career. She did the same thing after growing up in Pittsburgh, where most people chose to stay put, as they did in Wales. She put it simply: *'I was very curious – and I had the balls to see it through.'*

Amali de Alwis develops the idea further: *'You also need to look for multiple experiences – because experience can be biased too.'*

This section explores some of the keys to developing CQ by immersing yourself in experience.

An extra eye

Travelling helps, and I don't just mean geographically. You need to travel to places where the culture is different and open yourself up to it. Travel across generations: to schools and universities, and cut your talk down to a brief introduction and then open it up to discussion, so that you can learn. Travel to different parts of your community or city and see how different things look from there. See how a planning department deals with planning applications and warring parties in a city administration as they try to balance the impossible competing demands of neighbours, developers and politicians. Watch how a prison governor runs a prison, as they are sent all the people the city prefers to forget, with no clarity on whether the task is to punish, constrain or rehabilitate them. Attend a community group meeting where the task is to meet huge community needs on a shoestring while you try to keep your head down so that politicians don't think you're becoming too influential. See how a manufacturing plant controls its costs and finds the trained people to help it grow. Understand as a politician tries to make good long-term decisions, yet win the next election. Listen to a faith leader trying to hold their community together, with old and young wanting such different things. Or a banker, who knows how essential to society good banking is but needs to re-establish the trust that banking relies on. Study a school headteacher, and see how they run things when everyone in the world went to school, so they all think they know how to run it better than the headteacher does. And so on, and so on, and so on.

Discover the one consistent message the world over: the planners, neighbours, developers, politicians, production directors, faith leaders, bankers and headteachers hardly know one another, and very seldom make two and two make four.

And, of course, travel across the world, not just to see the sights but, as my South African colleague Elsbeth says, '*to smell the coffee – and to suck the lemons*'. The coffee because it makes you sit down and talk and sniff what is going on around you, and the lemons because they're bitter and uncomfortable; they smart in your mouth and the sensation stays with you for some time.

Gavin Dyer in Johannesburg puts it well: *'Most white South Africans in their forties, fifties and sixties will have a unique one-dimensional view, because they will not have been exposed to anything but the Afrikaner and English cultures in their childhood. They will likely have been to a white school and then a white university. They won't have experienced black or international cultures, unless they were immigrants or still had past contacts. I am pretty typical. In the late 1980s, when I started work, the ANC was still banned. My only CQ learning was on the shop floor, with blue-collar workers and shop stewards. So really I had zero CQ. I was a cultural moron. I started to open up, about five or six years on, when "Voter Education" began. And then I began to travel internationally: that's when everything started to shift for me.'* As a participant on the CSCLeaders programme, Gavin had the opportunity to do the second half of it in either Mumbai, which he knew little, or Johannesburg. Interestingly, he decided to stay in Joburg, because he thought he knew it even less: *'Now I want to travel in my own country more.'*

Also in Johannesburg, Di Schneider (who has always thought of herself as a traveller) is struggling: *'I was born a crossover person: I have always believed that I am a black person in a white skin, but put me in China, and I sink. To start with, I was huge, taller than anyone. I swear that everyone in the street was looking at me. I became incredibly self-conscious. I was lost, I wasn't me. I felt looked at, so I shut myself up. I became like Gulliver.'* She recalls one incident where she shocked herself: *'I got on a bus to go back to the hotel, but I got on the wrong one. When I realised it was going in the wrong direction, I panicked. So I marched up to the driver and showed him the address. He reacted to my stress by stressing himself. In the end, he threw me off the bus, shouting "you don't belong". I felt like an alien – and, to my shock, I behaved like one.'* But Di is determined: *'When I go back, I will try to do so with more warmth.'*

So travel: and make sure that you experience the experience when you get there.

However, I do have one small warning: make sure you get your re-entry right. Recently, I met a journalist in Berlin, and I asked her what it was like to be back in her home town after years of global journalism. Her reply surprised me: *'It's taking a while. I thought that I would be valued by my colleagues and neighbours for my global experience, because I had been to some tough parts of the world. Far from it. They pretty much all asked why I had been away at all. And they all wanted to know how I was going to prove myself again now that I was back.'*

Find the right guide

Wherever you travel, even in your own city, you will need good guides and plenty of them. The problem is, if you don't know where you are and you don't know what to look out for, how do you find a guide you trust? Because there are as many good ones as bad ones.

Back to Di Schneider in Johannesburg: *'I hate the township tours. All the gawking and the "ooohs" and "aaahs". And comments like "they even have curtains". I look for a guide with compassion, not knowledge, and you find it in their eyes. If they are nervous, their eyes will flicker when you speak. But, between the flickers, you will see it in their eyes.'*

Etienne de Villiers agrees: *'I remember holding a tennis tournament in China. A local guy who lived there kept telling everyone what to say and how to move. His whole life was based on this role, interpreting the local thing. It started as sweet, but it became sickening, because it wasn't genuine.'*

I laugh, partly out of shame. No question, some guides are just plain bad. They don't have compassion and they aren't genuine, and they can lead you into a lot of trouble. At university years ago, I had a friend who was Polish, and he deeply, deeply hated all things Russian. Then we were asked to look after some Russian visitors. To my surprise, my Polish friend immediately said yes. Then he started briefing me on what he planned to do. The naughtiest thing we did was introduce them to teabags. We sat carefully around a table, showed them how to receive their china cups of hot water, elegantly keeping their little fingers in the air, then how to open up their teabag and dunk it five times quickly in succession in the water, before lifting it up right above their heads and sucking it, chins sticking up in the air, Elegantly. I giggle as I remember the six Russians all sitting sucking their teabags. My Polish friend loved every minute. Superiority oozed out of him. The other people in the restaurant stared in amazement at first, then they started to giggle and point. How the university could have selected a Pole (him) and a fool (me) to show Russians around its campus remains a mystery. I know that I have been ashamed ever since. I have also been very cautious about etiquette – and choosing the right guides.

Many of the people I have spoken to about finding good guides have mentioned eyes. They seem crucial to the trust decision, and across different cultures too. It certainly works for me.

Albert Tucker is a Fairtrade pioneer from Sierra Leone. He gave me an interesting analogy from boxing. Not that I do much boxing, of course, but he says, '*In a boxing match, you must watch the eyes, not the fists. Watch the eyes and you will see what they are planning. So you will see the punch coming. Watch the fists and you will see it too late and you won't be able to protect yourself.*'

In the boxing ring or not, I think it's useful advice for choosing guides in unfamiliar cultures.

Finally, Vidya Shah in Mumbai gives a timely warning about travelling without guides at all:

'*There was a news story in 2012 about an Indian couple with two small children who were posted to Norway. The teachers at their child's school reported them for feeding the child by hand, which they equated with "force-feeding". Both children were taken into care, for seven months, and the parents narrowly escaped imprisonment. They had no idea that things were so different in Norway. I don't think this would have happened in the US, where there are many more from the Indian Diaspora who would have briefed them. I agree that we must not codify culture, but there are some lines which need to be known. Which, if you cross, you don't just risk being ostracised, but put in jail.*'

Have courageous conversations

I have already referred to Reuel Khoza's total clarity on the issue of standing up when you see cultural intolerance. He is equally clear that leaders must also be prepared to have what he calls 'courageous conversations'. He thinks they are essential: '*Conversations when you state your view, even if the atmosphere in the room is unwelcoming. I mean conversations, not debates. Debates tend to lead you to take a hard stand. Conversations are preferable: because they play on the borders between Core and Flex.*'

Konstantin Mettenheimer agrees. In the same breath, he gives me both encouragement and a warning, because you can get to some very difficult topics: 'Wars, for example, make things particularly complicated. If you are German, the war, and with it the Holocaust, are very, very difficult subjects. They are complicated for us, because we cannot be proud of being German with any ease. Because, when we meet each other, we wonder what our fathers and grandfathers did in the war, and if they were Nazis. And, of course, half the German population lost their homes and were displaced, so the whole country was dislocated, and still is. Other countries suffered, lost family, saw terrible things, because of Germany. It is a very difficult subject, with deep undercurrents. Will it ever settle? I don't know. I have a friend who says that it will take seven generations. We have had only three generations so far.'

There are very difficult subjects to touch on everywhere. In Vietnam, Japan, Spain, Russia and all over Africa. Konstantin's advice? 'Don't back off, but be cautious. If the subject comes up and is the elephant under or on the table, then you have to name it and talk about it. But, when you do, be aware of all the people in the room. All are likely to have a story, many will say nothing and you will have to be strong to keep going. Don't make stupid jokes – and don't be casual. The past has to inform us. To use Reuel Khoza's good analogy, you should not drive with something covering your rear-view mirror, so that you don't have to look at the past. Yes, you must look forward, but every now and then, it is useful to take a clear, focused glimpse in the mirror.'

Former soldier Mike Martin's life seems to have consisted of one courageous conversation after another. While he was in Afghanistan, he produced an oral history of Helmand province, and what he discovered was a quite different way of looking at the region: 'In the West, we tend to think of the recent history of Afghanistan as a series of different ideological chapters – 1978–89: Mujahideen; 1989–94: civil war; 1994–2001: the Taliban; 2001–present: Western involvement. But, to the local people, it is one continuous story, over land or water, or blood lines . . . the same players or their families switch ideologies and roles at different times, depending on local political expediency. It is a pragmatic war, not an ideological one.'

Like a lot of the journey towards CQ, courageous conversation can be difficult, but it can also challenge received wisdom and your own assumptions, and make you see something afresh.

Switch from transmit to receive

This was one of my father's favourite expressions. From two-way radio communications, it means turning the dial so that you stop talking and have to listen. Michael Hastings makes the same point in a different way: '*Sometimes, I think there is real value in entering someone else's drama. Put away your story and enter theirs.*'

Robert Care at Arup in Australia says part of the skill of this is coping with silence: '*I have learnt – slowly and sometimes quite painfully – to observe. To remain silent in the gap. Most Westerners find this very difficult to do, because they want to fill the silence with noise. And, even when they listen, they have their reply in the pipeline long before the other person has stopped talking. I do it too, but I try very hard not to.*'

My daughter Emma is in her twenties and she still can't bear silence. She starts to fidget nervously and then babble, just to fill it. It is almost agony for her not to fill the silence. As a family, we tease her and lay bets on how long she will last. Almost the same age, Dalisu Jwara, studying in Cape Town, sees this as a real problem: '*The trouble is that the advantaged are so confident and loud. How do you make disadvantaged leaders have the confidence to speak up, if the others will not be quiet?*'

In my daughter's case, the dislike of silence translates into noise to fill it. But Dalisu makes a good point: silence does not automatically mean disengagement, and we shouldn't assume that it means agreement either. Sometimes the silent need encouragement to talk. Sometimes they just need everyone else to be quiet.

And it doesn't get any better with age. Issa Baluch, now in his sixties, tells me: '*I have lived in Africa for 20 years, and then in the Middle East for 35 years, and now I have lived in the US for four years. I do struggle. And the biggest struggle is with speaking up. I can't get used to saying anything you like, boldly disagreeing with anyone you want, from your neighbour to your government. I have little experience of speaking my mind without fear, and sometimes it means that I can't enter a debate. Conversely, US citizens cannot get their heads around the fact that they cannot do this everywhere.*'

Leaders need to be aware of this and do something about it, because otherwise, as Philip Yang says, you just miss what is really going on in the room: '*Chinese people can appear quite introverted. We are quiet. We even smile quietly. But we can keep on smiling and listening, when in our hearts all trust is lost. If you talk too much, you miss the opportunity to know what we know. If you ask questions, you might get answers. Chinese people know quite a lot of things, but you have to elicit them.*'

If you don't switch to receive, you miss CQ learning opportunities. Genevieve Barr (who is, after all, deaf herself) says she does it too. She gave me an example of a young man on the disabled leaders' course she runs: '*He is a paraplegic, who has now graduated from university. He can move his arms a little – enough to eat and to write – and he has a severe speech impediment. All through the programme, he was patient, wrote a lot of notes on his iPad and spoke very little. On the last day, the participants were very confident and throwing questions out. He had been trying to raise his hand but, with his limited mobility, was struggling to get noticed. He had spoken so little over the three days that his presence was easy to overlook. The speaker, Ruth, who is also deaf and was using an interpreter, picked up on his efforts. I didn't. When she invited him to put his question, he then asked, "How do you communicate when people don't want to listen?" It triggered a discussion which will remain in all our minds. So much so that, months later at a follow-up event, he led the entire presentation. He was the only one to speak. It took 15 minutes longer, but the time stood still: no one in the room blinked an eye while he was talking. I think the quietest voices in the room are the ones you should maybe put your confidence in.*'

Bella in Zimbabwe is not quiet; she never has been and I doubt she ever will be. I saw her give an impromptu talk at the end of an event recently that made your heart sing. But, when she went to Mumbai with Common Purpose, she saw something very different: '*I simply could not believe the quiet, simple demeanour of the leader from the Tata Group who spoke to us. A man who has had such success, who is an intellectual, who is crisp and analytical. His demeanour was amazing as he opened himself up to the barrage of questions we threw at him. I am used to puffed-up leaders who behave like peacocks. Yet here was a man telling a very simple story of turning round one company after another, in a simple, quiet, subtle and smart way. It taught me that the very best of leaders know when to be quiet. And I said to myself that, from now on, I will watch them.*'

Perhaps it's like choosing the right guides. It's in the eyes, and it's also in the silences: when you learn to let them happen.

Open the door

Dalisu in Cape Town told me a lovely story: '*My grandmother would invite people into our small meagre house in the township, and share what she had. A man arrived one day who had come from Durban by boat. He was from Liberia. When he arrived at our gate, he was swollen and he asked for water. My grandmother treated him like her own son. Her instinct was to always open her door to other people, and she would want to hear their story. People always wanted to be heard, so they would tell it to her, and I would hear it too.*'

For Dalisu, it was his grandmother's commitment to opening the door that started to give him CQ. For her, it was a literal act of welcoming strangers and hearing their stories. For me, it is also a simple, useful metaphor for much of what this book is about.

When you open the door, others can come in and you can go out. It's physical, it's mental and it's sensory. It applies at home and at work. It's a generous act, and it is often a decision that you make in an instant (like the decision to say something when you hear cultural intolerance).

The challenge is to open the door and not get bad-tempered when something unfamiliar comes through it. Gavin Dyer in Johannesburg puts it very well: '*The African culture is loud. Loud and noisy. People laugh louder, clap louder, move noisily, dance loudly, shout louder, squeal louder, eat louder. Some people can't cope with it, or even judge it harshly. Now, I see it as saying, "I have nothing to hide." There are no whispered conversations here.*'

The other challenge is to go out through the door yourself, and do it with confidence.

There is an alternative, of course, and many people choose it. To leave the door locked, and stay behind it.

Scenario: Advice for leaders leaving home

Much of this is easy to agree with in principle but rather harder to put into practice. So I asked the people I've been talking to about CQ to give me some advice for leaders from their part of the world who are about to go and work in another one. Here is what they said:

Issa Baluch – Boston

I have two small pieces of advice for young US citizens when they travel abroad:

1. In the West, when you turn 18 you become an adult, overnight. And in the year up to your 18th birthday, you have been preparing for the day. It's not like this in most of the rest of the world.

2. You need to understand the culture and you need to understand the law too. People tend to forget this. Even if it is just Canada, you can't enter if you have had a DUI (driving under the influence) conviction in the last 10 years. Young people look stunned when something stops them in their tracks over which they have no control. Similarly, if you travel to Dubai, you can't just say anything you want there.

Alan Rosling – Mumbai

What advice would I give to a young Indian manager who is about to lead a team in the West?

1. Listen. In India, you are trained to think that the leader should know all the answers. People come to Indian leaders with their problems to ask for solutions, and that's what Indian leaders tend to give them. In

the West, people often bring their own proposed solutions. This is not a show of disrespect: it's empowerment. If they don't have solutions and just bring you a problem, your role should not be to give them your solution; but rather to elicit the solution out of them.

2. Don't deny who you are: don't drop your Core so as to integrate too fast. If you try too hard, you will be seen as a crank.

3. Remember how bad Westerners are when they are in India. Don't do the same. Don't be arrogant. Don't tell people how you do things.

4. Be confident. Indians are incredible adaptors, because their country is so diverse. They have been invaded by languages, cultures and armies over the years. As a result, they are tolerant of difference like no others. And they succeed all over the world and get to the top wherever they are.

Lady Susan Rice – Edinburgh

In much of the Anglo-Saxon world, we welcome those who speak up. Directness carries a value to us, but maybe not to every audience, especially if we haven't stopped first to listen. If one's instinct in a new situation, and especially in a different culture, is to amplify the characteristic of speaking up and speaking first, beware. Take a bit of time to listen or establish a personal connection first. Showing off can too easily be seen as showing up.

Even within the English-speaking world, words have different meanings in different countries. I remember early on after I moved to Scotland, asking someone to put a report in one of my drawers as I rushed out, and later on saying something about scrubbing data. Two of several instances where I brought blushes to everyone in earshot, because these words are often used in an off-colour way here, but I had no idea.

What makes us laugh varies widely in different cultures. Irony and double takes are a common aspect of communication in the Anglo-Saxon world. However good an English vocabulary people from another part of the world may have, don't assume they all 'get' the cheeky comment, the cynical aside, the double take. It helps to do a sense check: 'back home what I just said really means . . .' Or share one of your own cultural misunderstandings, which shows you can laugh at yourself and gives your listeners permission to make a similar mistake themselves.

We see ourselves through the lens of others. I'm a businessperson and a banker, someone who provides support for the arts, who tries to influence in the areas of financial inclusion, environmental matters and climate justice. But, as I've become more senior, many people and especially women have tried to draw on my being the first or the only woman in particular roles. In a completely different culture and country, however, what likely stands out is that I'm from the UK, or originally the US, and that I know how things are done in those countries. Over time, we become aware of how others see us in our normal work environments, which means you have to take extra care to understand that our national identity, for instance, may be the dominant factor in a different environment. It's important to try to find out how others value you when you're in a different culture, and not make assumptions.

In the Anglo-Saxon world, we don't often hesitate when we need to say 'no' – to a question, a proposition, whatever. We might explain why, but we're clear and direct in our response and expect others to be. However, in some places, people are uncomfortable saying 'no'. So you have to be able to spot when there's no real 'yes'. A colleague once told me that if I say 'that's interesting' when listening to an idea around my executive team table, it actually means that I've lost interest. In other cultures, we have to be able to spot their version of 'that's interesting'.

I was recently in Suzhou in China with colleagues. We were waiting for a train and noticed that the others waiting, all of whom were Chinese, were standing in a queue, just as we were. But, when the train arrived, while we intended to board our carriage as always in an orderly fashion, everyone else broke out of their queues, creating a good deal of mayhem as they boarded. Whether we're living in a different country, or in a meeting with people from different nationalities, everyone may know what 'the rules' are, but don't assume we follow them in the same way, or indeed at all. The UK typically follows them. Other countries may treat the rules more as guidelines, to put it discreetly, or interpret them altogether differently. So keep your eye on what you want to achieve, but don't assume yours is the only way to get there.

Martin Kalungu-Banda – Zambia

My advice to an African leader who is making the transition to a global role?

1. Be curious about things, even things you (inwardly) violently disagree with. Ask questions so that you understand. Then try out the new ways (as long as you're not doing anything illegal), even if it means fighting with your Core. I deeply regret the time that I wasted at the outset when I came to the UK pretending to listen and then rushing home to download how awful everything was. If you have moved to a place, take an interest in it. Why go there otherwise? And if you don't, you just get more grumpy. I thought it was horrible how people held hands and even kissed in public. But then I started to ask myself: is this grumpy person who I really am?

2. Draw on a saying which came from my tribe, which was a fisherman's tribe. It was advice they gave you if you were going to another village: 'Keep your net in your house'. Basically, keep out of sight, see how the locals do their fishing first. Don't arrive and tell them all how to fish, even if (or especially if) you are an amazing fisherman. And, if people visit because they have heard about you and they ask to see your net, say 'it is being mended at the moment'. Don't be tempted to bring it out. Let your new environment rub on you, before you rub on it. When you do eventually bring out your net, do it quietly, when no one is watching, and slip it gently into the river. And, if you have any thoughts about the best place to put your nets, keep them to yourself at first. When you do start to say, 'I think that might be a good place', expect the locals to disagree at first. If you localise yourself by 'keeping your net in the house', you will adapt in days, rather than months. Soon they will all be asking you where to fish.

Seiji Shiraki – Brazil

My advice to someone Japanese going for their first big international job? (Note: I don't call it a global job; to me, 'global' is an artificial word coined by American businessmen who want a new frontier for their global markets. It is a world in which there are no identities, and it does not exist. I am international, with my own culture, which is itself enriched by access to other cultures.)

1. Keep firmly in your mind that you have been given the chance to travel. This is a privilege for which you should be grateful. It is not a burden. Be delighted – and express your delight.

2. Respect wherever it is you go.

3. Get as much information as you can about the new country, even if it is a country which does not like Japan. I went to Korea in 1979, at a time when we had many Koreans who did not like the Japanese. Many people said some very harsh things to me when I was there. I made sure that every morning when I woke up, I looked in the mirror and very deliberately said to myself, 'What can I do for Korea today?' It reminded me that I was adding value, not just to my company, but also to Korea in my work. It also reminded me that I was human and so were the Koreans, and that we would find a way to work together eventually.

But really, you should ask the opposite question: what advice would you give to a Japanese leader as they return to Japan from being an international leader? This is more difficult. My son and daughter – who had been to international schools and learnt CQ – found the prospect of returning very difficult. My daughter is now back in Japan, and her boyfriend is English. My son's wife is half-German, and they are about to go and live in Germany. I have a mix of cultures even in my own family, which I am really enjoying. I myself keep a clear identity – and try to be a good Samurai. In the 21st century, Samurais need to have an international mindset.

Philip Yang – Tianjin

My advice to Chinese professionals going to work in the West? First of all is the entertainment. After a business meeting or work, the team agrees to have dinner. In China, it is a relatively simple process. We go to the restaurant to enjoy the tea and share the dinner with beer or wine. On many occasions, the team will have a private dining room. Sometimes in the private room, they even have karaoke. We stay there all evening. But in the West, people like to change the environments. They will go to a pub to have beer for a while, then go to a restaurant for a dinner with beer or wine and then, after dinner, they will go to a bar to continue to have beer or wine. The reason for the difference? It's probably because we Chinese really focus on the 'hard' thing: food, tea, wine, and Western people focus on the 'soft' thing: the environment, the conversations, etc.

The second thing is about hospitality. If you, as a guest, come to visit China, I as your host will attend to every detail to receive you: logistics, dinner, I will go to the hotel to say hello, and so on. But when I travel to the West, I learned that I should not have this kind of expectation. Western people are more independent and respect privacy. So they normally will let us look after ourselves.

Maria Figueroa Kupcu – New York

My advice to Americans who get posted outside the US:

1. Resist the 'if there is a problem, there is a solution' default position. Accept that some problems don't have solutions. Or, at least, that the solution does not have to come from you.

2. Teach yourself to do a double take: what you are hearing may not be what was meant. Conversely, maybe it *was* meant, so you are going to have to get used to hearing things that you are not trained to hear. You must overcome your cultural baggage, and listen.

Vandana Saxena Poria – Pune

My advice to Indians who travel abroad to work for the first time is to turn all your thinking about authority on its head. Let me explain. You have to understand the depth of the issues about authority in India. Only one generation ago, authority and power was absolute. When my father was seven, my grandmother's sister had a stillborn baby. So my grandmother sent him 'on loan' to her for a few years. When I asked my father how he felt about this, he looked startled and replied that this was simply what happened and there was nothing to 'feel' about it.

Go to any Indian market and see how a stall boss – sitting cross-legged on a cushion, set on a platform – treats his skivvies, whom he will call 'beta' (son) even though they are mostly significantly older than him (and guess how the 'beta' treats his own family when he goes home in the evening). Such hierarchy is endemic: it's not on paper, it's in the head. This means that when a young Indian takes a job outside India, my first advice is: don't expect respect until you have earned it – the family you come from, or the caste that you are, will have no bearing outside of India. Also if you want anyone to do anything, don't expect them to take your word for it: you have to tell them why.

Conclusion

In writing this book, I have discovered some powerful new images, which have now gone into my Core, to join the many that my father put in there long ago (like the fear of becoming one of the Flying Dead).

Reuel Khoza's 'rear-view mirror' is now rooted in me. I have long struggled with the past. In my own three circles, the past has always been tiny; the present is a little bit less tiny than the past (but not much); and the future is vast and full of Hope (with a capital H). I think the concept of the rear-view mirror might have changed this for me. I love Reuel's driving position: looking forwards, but with an eye to the rear-view mirror. As a leader myself, I find this is helpful, and also for my Cultural Intelligence: in many cultures, the past features so strongly that its tininess for me (and my resulting discounting of it generally) is a barrier to my own CQ.

On the whole, I treat people exactly the same: this is both an asset and a weakness. It is perhaps why so many people have told me so much while I've been writing this book. It could also explain why so many people I admire are not 20 but 30 years younger than me. It is a huge strength, and it's deep in my Core. But Mike Brearley has put something in there alongside it. I think I probably excel at troubling the comfortable, but I am not sure that I do enough to comfort the troubled, especially the troubled from other cultures, whom I don't spot as troubled, probably because I treat all people exactly the same.

So, as I complete the book, I find myself feeling a bit shocked; having to rethink my own history and that of my country of birth; pretty embarrassed by moments when I have (if only figuratively) driven in the bus lane; and feeling the same about meetings I have had that I judged quickly and wrongly, and which I would like to go back to and do again. Quite a few multi-sector meetings ('tri-sector', to use Arun's word), and some in Asia Pacific which I left, convinced that we had reached agreement, and now look back on and realise that people were probably just being polite.

I am also disappointed by the tendency of much of the world to judge people by their accent and demeanour and birth, rather than what they say and do, and worried that, though I tell myself that I will be more quiet, I am not sure that I will succeed. (Although I do think that I will think differently about others when they appear quiet.)

I anticipate many more courageous (and probably some foolhardy) conversations ahead. Armed as I am now with more clarity about things, I want to talk to more leaders from other countries – especially from cultures I don't know. As Common Purpose grows across the world, I intend to learn more.

When I started writing this book, I knew CQ was important. Now I've finished, I think I underestimated it.

I think CQ will define the winners: the winning leaders; the winning cultures; the winning cities and countries. What will cause them to thrive and ultimately succeed will be their ability not simply to cope with, but fully to benefit from, the heterogeneous nature of organisations and society.

But, for the most part, I fear they will still be going against the grain, because, in the aftermath of the kind of economic turmoil we have been going through globally, societies turn in on themselves, and wars erupt.

The large parts of the world that go with the grain will continue to judge people before they have opened their mouths, blame all of society's problems on whichever sector they do not work in, put young people at the other end of the table at dinner and get the usual suspects together to address the same old problems. So talent will continue to be wasted, and resources will continue to be squandered on trying to paper over the divides.

Technology will play its part for sure, in all ways. It will make the world gloriously more interconnected. It will make boundaries meaningless. But, if we're not careful, it will only provide a veneer of cultural understanding. Leaders who cannot meet the new interconnectedness with

CQ will struggle. Leaders who try to re-establish boundaries – and the institutions that go with them – will be marginalised. Leaders who don't go deeper than the polite veneer (as they loftily talk of being 'Citizens of the Net') will fail to build the deeper relationships and real trust they will need to succeed.

All this will present a huge opportunity for people who choose another route. To inhabit and lead in the places where the sectors have had enough of conflict and decide to overcome their differences instead. In the places where the talent across the world – from all cultures, backgrounds, generations – will gather.

Leaders who develop CQ will have done so through experience: painful and sometimes humiliating experience, generously offered to them by others. The experience will have led them not to understand all cultures (this would be an impossible task), but to find CQ in themselves or, at least, to unpick the barriers to CQ that lie inside them.

They will have established the difference between their Core and Flex, holding the two alongside each other, and in the same beat, because this is where CQ lies. They will be moving the dividing line between the two with great caution, but move it they will, largely keeping to their Core and, crucially, Flexing their Flex. They will be starting to use the vocabulary of Core and Flex to explain things to themselves, and to understand others. Recently, someone asked me about my trip to Jeddah (in that intemperate way, emphasising the word 'they'): '*If you were prepared to Flex in your dress when you went to Jeddah, why can't they do the same when they come to London?*' For me, the answer was simpler now: '*I don't care how I dress, I never have; it is firmly in my Flex. But, for many women in Jeddah, how they dress is in their Core.*' My questioner looked at me for a long while, and digested. Then she nodded, and said, '*OK*'.

I have learned that CQ is littered with loose ends. And balancing acts. And unanswerable questions.

How do you get enough CQ for people to trust you with their stories, so that you can then develop CQ? How much intolerance should you tolerate? Are you really suggesting that I make a stand when I see cultural ignorance or intolerance – in an instant, a moment loaded with promise and danger – when I am terrified that I am setting myself up in judgement, that I will make the atmosphere more awkward, and probably worse?

The danger is that these questions are just so tough that we don't even go there. We stay away and keep quiet (like so many from my generation have). But if we take that easy option, things will fester, mistrust will continue and opportunities will be missed. The judgements just have to be made.

It is the job of a leader to square circles. Maybe in CQ, you simply have some of the trickiest circles to square. The judgements have to be made by leaders using their CQ, leaders who have mastered the most difficult culture of all: their own.

The prize is that you won't be one of the Flying Dead: the leaders who my father predicted would fail to deliver on the promise that, as the world got smaller, it would become more coherent. Instead of becoming the world's natural bridge-builders, they would merely become its ghosts, carrying their blindness – or worse, their intolerance – around the world with them, flying economy as well as business class (because the Flying Dead are everywhere).

Instead of that fate, you'll become a leader around whom the whole is greater than the sum of the parts; a leader who young people want to work with, and women, and men, and leaders from other sectors, and Africans, and Asians, and Europeans, and, and, and . . . Innovation will happen around you, resources will be cleverly used wherever you are, complex problems will be cracked and boundaries – old and new – will be confidently swept aside.

And, in truth, not everything is complicated or messy. There are some very simple messages for leaders in search of CQ: help the people you lead to pin down their Core – good and bad – and to air it on a regular basis, and demand – outright – that Flex gets Flexed (as you Flex yours), because this is the point of it.

Ultimately, I think CQ is about openness; a refusal to lock yourself in your own culture, behind a door you refuse to open; a belief that other cultures will enrich yours rather than dilute it; a willingness to use all encounters – whether helpful or grim – to build your CQ.

What would a world filled with culturally intelligent leaders look like? It would avoid divergence, and it would refute convergence, on the grounds that it is neither possible nor desirable. Is there such a thing as co-vergence? And, if not, could we create it? Getting the strength from many cultures without drowning any out? Getting two and two to make ten? I hope so.

Love Julia

PS Don't forget to send me your thoughts on what I have not understood or what I have missed out.

cqforJulia@commonpurpose.org

Over to you

To develop CQ you have to go out and get some. So here are two techniques that might help. One is a scenario I developed with a very successful (and very tall) American CEO, in a discussion about how you make sure you use all the talent in an organisation. The other is a way of introducing CQ into your (and your organisation's) assessment process. I think they're interesting. I hope they're also useful.

Scenario: 100 people in a room

Put 100 people in a room. Separate them into two corners, using whatever criteria you want (tall and short, men and women, chew gum or don't chew gum, it doesn't matter).

Now bring two leaders into the room. Tell them that they must both recruit a team from the people in the room to perform an identical complex task. The first leader can recruit from only one corner of the room. The second leader can recruit from both corners of the room.

Now answer these two questions:

1. What would you say to persuade people that the second leader will get the higher-performing team?

2. What advice would you give the second leader about leading the team in such a way that the members don't start to slide back into their original corners?

I put these questions to several of the people I've spoken to while I've been writing this book. Here are some of the answers they gave me to the first question:

Amali de Alwis – Thought Leadership Consultant

The second leader will have a greater pool of talent to pick from. This outweighs the early benefits of having a team that starts with something in common. However, if the leader doing the selection prefers (or can only judge) people who are like them, then they may still pick a team made up of people who are too similar to each other, and therefore miss out on talent in the room.

Mark Huang – US venture capitalist

Group-think is, unfortunately, a natural human trait. Perhaps, in a primal sense, human evolution all goes back to people behaving as herd-like animals. But people of different cultural backgrounds or simply different life experiences can provide input and ideas that conventional thought typically dismisses. It is hard for a group to 'think outside of the box' when the whole group has been together for a while. So the second team will have an edge in terms of innovation.

Anu Omideyi – British barrister

I'm not sure why I would have to persuade anyone – because it is obvious, assuming that the two leaders are choosing at the same time, so that the second leader isn't choosing 'leftovers'. I wonder if part of the problem is that a more diverse team is considered to include 'leftovers'. There will always be people who mutter in some way about 'positive discrimination diluting the quality': they are almost always lazy, and/or disingenuous. The idea that somewhere, there isn't a minority who more than match the standard of the majority is sheer nonsense. Then again, it is a reality that many of the most talented minorities have long since stopped putting themselves forward just to be rejected.

Lady Susan Rice – Managing Director, Lloyds Banking Group

The first leader with a team who share a particular characteristic – especially if it's easily perceived – will have a team in which there is at least a tacit assumption that their individual value lies in what is common to them all. That, in turn, might serve to reinforce the view that their judgement is the right judgement, so long as it is shared. Members might also pay close attention to the judgements of the others on the team, to ensure that there is indeed such alignment: because implicit in the situation is that the people around the table must have the correct judgement. It will also be a team in which it is more difficult for one member to offer a contrary view. It would not be expected of them – because the probability is that they're all on the team because they are similar. So a contrary view might be initially discounted as not being credible or immediately acceptable. That view would have a hurdle to get over before it was actually considered, if at all, on its own merits.

I take the view that the second leader will have a diverse team in which it is anticipated (indeed expected) that different members will have different views. Each member will perhaps have a bit more confidence about offering their own perspective, because there are fewer unspoken obstacles to doing so, and, possibly, also because they may perceive they are expected to tell their particular 'story'.

Both models have inherent difficulties, but the first leader perhaps has the greater challenge. That individual needs to understand that it's rare that one person has the best idea, and that most good ideas are shaped and reshaped by a shared discourse, and by eclectic experience and thinking entering into that discourse. A team which has individuals who are diverse in background, in experience and, indeed, in appearance, will make it much more likely that a range of views will be aired.

Here is a selection of the answers they gave me to the second question:

Anu Omideyi

For me, everything is results-led. So I'd always be working backwards from my desired finishing point – and working very hard to exceed it. The question of diversity is, therefore, only relevant insofar as I would expect it as a necessity to achieve my ends. It wouldn't be the other way round; diversity is not the end itself.

Susan Rice

My advice to the second leader would be to ensure that they create an environment where absolutely everyone's voice can be heard, where people listen as well as speak and where the nature of the discourse is based on constructive challenge, perhaps by asking a lot of questions. Asking someone more and more focused questions about the reasons for or background to their view will help everyone around the table to understand it, including the holder of the view, and will help the group feel comfortable if they decide to take that particular perspective forward. It's important that people listen in this diverse team, because the members may be more likely to want to have their voice heard, rather than checking out what others might think to see if it's aligned with their own view.

Olu Olanrewaju – CEO of a British housing association

From the word go, the leader must recognise that they have to work hard to maximise the potential of the diverse group. The leader has to create an environment in which differences can be openly discussed; look for dissent; bring to the open the elephants in the room; set very clear ground rules; ensure every voice counts; continually go on about what binds the group together (which is to complete the complex task); and, lastly, role-model the behaviour they expect from the team. Then the leader must continually celebrate what binds the team together, as well as what is so different amongst them.

Graham Boyce – former ambassador

In my experience, it's better to overlay a pattern of behaviours rather than a culture, otherwise, you can kill the different cultures that should be the team's strength. I once had a boss who put up a notice: 'From tomorrow, the following traditions will come into effect'. He was well loved by all and, somehow, they became the team's common traditions. They were small things, like having lunch together once a month, and using different coloured inks to give each other feedback on papers. They were quick and easy to do – and they didn't interfere with the many cultures within the team, which remained intact.

Amali de Alwis

Proactively drive people to work across teams. Difference is less scary once people get to know each other and start to find a very simple common ground. I recently saw an interview with conductor Daniel Barenboim, who was talking about building trust between Israeli and Palestinian musicians in his orchestra. He said it was best to find common ground: in this case, music. He did not need political consensus: a consensus on Beethoven was enough for him. Then you must create a safe environment where people trust you not to shoot them down, just because they think differently. The stronger the trust, the more willing people are to stick their necks out.

Ben Burnand – Country Manager at Anglo American, Singapore

Three things:

1. You have to connect with people. Do the solid, important, old-fashioned things: take time to understand people, who they are and where they are coming from. Really listen to what they are saying and show respect for their unique points of view. Take time to understand a little bit about their context, what has influenced their lives and how this manifests in their various idiosyncrasies. Through this open discovery, seek out things you have in common and use them to connect. My go-to topic is typically music; while there are definitely different tastes, the power of music seems to transcend boundaries and doesn't need as much translation (though I must admit to being caught out with my Chinese colleagues, where no one has heard of any of my favourite bands!).

2. Energise people: innately, people the world over follow and/or support the person with a plan or who is optimistic about possible outcomes.

3. Shape rather than direct. The power of diverse groups is achieved by creating a space or platform for collaboration and creativity, rather

than a need to be the 'boss'. Establishing this 'safe' space is key. Open up the conversations about difficult things. Challenge people to talk; and, in so doing, widen the issues that people are prepared to talk about. Don't be scared to talk about things like racism and prejudice, and do it from every angle, including racism towards majorities. The intention is to create confidence that we can talk about the difficult topics and reduce the amount of corridor gossiping or moaning – adopt a 'manage rather than moan' culture. All people want to be heard, respected and supported. As long as this is in place, they don't always need to be agreed with. Establishing this understanding amongst the team does not solve the really challenging problems that might be thrown your way, but it will establish in all team members' minds how, as a team, the problem will be dealt with. Consistency allows everyone to work through how they can contribute to resolving issues and dealing with outcomes that might not be their preferred solution.

Di Schneider – HR Director, South Africa

If the leader has low CQ, it is probably better for them to lead team one, the more homogeneous team. Remember, very few leaders do have CQ. Let's face it, not that many can stride into a room, mingle and connect.

Exercise: Eight Poles: assess your CQ

You can't analyse your own CQ. You have to ask other leaders to help. Leaders who know or work with you, and who will tell you the truth. Eight Poles is not unlike a 360-degree assessment. Just broader and more open-ended. You ask leaders who are poles apart for feedback on your CQ.

To start with, identify eight leaders who are very different from you (or you can start with four and work up to eight).

NORTH:
A leader from a different **Generation**, at least 20 years older or younger than you.

SOUTH:
A leader whose perspective will come from a place over **7,000 km** from you.

EAST:
A leader with a different **Faith** from you.

WEST:
A leader who works in a different **Sector** from you (Public, Private or NGO).

NORTH WEST:
A leader born with different perceived **Prospects** from you.

NORTH EAST:
A leader who isn't your **Gender**.

SOUTH EAST:
A leader who has different **Politics** from you.

SOUTH WEST:
A leader with significantly less or more experience of **Disability** than you.

The first four

North: A leader from a different **Generation**, at least 20 years older or younger than you.

South: A leader whose perspective will come from a place over **7,000 km** from you.

East: A leader with a different **Faith** from you.

West: A leader who works in a different **Sector** from you (public, private or NGO).

Then four more

North West: A leader born with different perceived **Prospects** from you.

North East: A leader who isn't your **Gender**.

South East: A leader who has different **Politics** from you.

South West: A leader with significantly less or more experience of **Disability** than you.

Whether you start with the four or the eight poles, ask the leaders you have identified the same set of 16 questions and then listen carefully to their answers (both what they say and what they don't say).

If you can't identify a candidate for each of the eight poles, then start with one or two. Finding the others will become part of your CQ journey.

The sixteen questions

1. Do you think this person is interested in other cultures?

2. Does this person have many friends or colleagues who are like you?

3. Have you ever seen this person stumble in a new culture?

4. Please underline who you think this person feels very comfortable being with (underline as many as you like):

- public/private/NGO sectors
- own generation/people younger than them/people older than them
- people of same faith/ people of any faith/people with no faith
- people of same politics/people of different politics/people of no politics
- people from own country/people from own continent/people from any continent
- men/women/people of different sexual orientation
- able-bodied/disabled

5. You are going to a difficult meeting involving people with whom you have a lot in common. Would you confidently take this person along with you, knowing that they will be in a minority of one?

6. Have you ever sensed this person pull back when meeting people?

7. Do you think this person would say something if they came across cultural intolerance?

8. Have you ever seen this person recover well from a situation involving someone very different which at first they misjudged?

9. Is this person actively interested in the views and ideas of people who are very different?

10. Have you seen this person's interest in people who are very different increase or decrease over time?

11. Would you describe this person as someone who is open to 'courageous conversations'?

12. Do you think that this person reveals enough of themselves to others?

13. Would you describe this person as confident about their own beliefs, values and behaviours?

14. Does this person take time to understand etiquette, and mostly get it right?

15. Have you ever seen this person impose their own culture on others?

And there's one very important final question:

16. Has knowing this person increased your own CQ?

If you would prefer to run this assessment process online, please visit www.commonpurpose.org/cq

Further reading

Altbach, Philip G., Liz Reisberg and Laura E. Rumbley. *Trends in Global Higher Education: Tracking an Academic Revolution*. Paris: United Nations Educational, Scientific and Cultural Organisation, 2009.

Denslow, Lanie and Allyson Stewart-Allen. *Working with Americans*. Harlow: Pearson Education Limited, 2002.

Gardner, Howard. *Frames of Mind: The Theory of Multiple Intelligences*. New York: Basic Books, 1983.

Goleman, Daniel. *Emotional Intelligence*. London: Bloomsbury Publishing, 1996.

Index